PARISH PASTORAL COUNCILS

William Dalton

PARISH PASTORAL COUNCILS:
A HANDBOOK

Including a Formation Course for Members

THE COLUMBA PRESS
DUBLIN 1990

THE COLUMBA PRESS
93, The Rise, Mount Merrion, Blackrock, Co Dublin, Ireland

First edition 1989
This Revised and Enlarged Edition 1990
Cover by Bill Bolger
Origination by The Columba Press
Printed in Ireland by
Genprint Ltd, Dublin.

ISBN 1 85607 009 3

Nihil Obstat:
James Dollard B.D., Lic. Hist. Eccl.
Imprimatur:
✠ Laurence Forristal
September 20th 1990

Acknowledgements:
This book has grown out of talks to groups of priests and lay people over the past three years. Some of the material has already appeared in my articles in *The Furrow* (March and May 1988) and in the Canadian review, *Studia Canonica*, 1988.

I am grateful to the Ossory Council of Priests for giving me the initial impetus to provide some guidelines for parish pastoral councils in the diocese, and to the Ossory Pastoral Group for their interest and encouragement. I am particularly indebted to Declan O'Brien, former chairman of the Irish Commission for the Laity, for his careful reading of the manuscript and his helpful suggestions.

Contents

Foreword

The Second Vatican Council, as it said in its very first document, *The Constitution on the Sacred Liturgy*, 'set out to impart an ever-increasing vigour to the Christian life of the faithful'. Thus, it was essentially a ***pastoral*** council.

Over the past twenty-five years, all those concerned with the pastoral life have been forced to examine and re-examine their views on matters such as the role of the Church, the place of the parish, the ministry of the ordained priest, the significance of baptism, pastoral theory and practice, the vocation of the baptised and the need for consultation.

At first, some may have regarded these matters as merely theoretical and somewhat peripheral to our established practices and parish structures. With a renewed interest in the New Testament and Christology, more are now convinced that such concepts must be accepted if we are to live as the People of God in a Christian community.

In 1986, the Irish Bishops, in their Emmaus Meeting, saw that the establishment of parish pastoral councils, in the spirit of the Second Vatican Council, would be a means of giving practical expression to many of these concepts and of involving all the faithful, priests, religious and laity, in the life and mission of the Church.

More recently, Pope John Paul II, in *Christifideles Laici*, brought all these elements together and recognised that 'the ecclesial community, while always having a universal dimension, finds its most immediate and visible expression in the ***parish***. It is there that the Church is seen locally.'

Last year, Father William Dalton published a handbook entitled, 'Parish Pastoral Councils'. The fact that it is no longer available testifies to the eagerness of so many people to carry out the wishes of their Pope and their pastors.

The handbook is now re-issued, considerably enlarged and updated. Father Dalton has combined his theoretical knowledge as a teacher at home and in Africa with his pastoral experience at home and in the United States. His book should continue to be a help to all who want to make the Church and the parish a place 'where everyone feels involved, wanted and loved.'

✠ *Laurence Forristal*
Bishop of Ossory

Introduction

Ever since the Second Vatican Council, the Church has been experiencing a surge of theological reflection on its own nature and identity. For the past two decades now, we have been hearing about the new ecclesiology and the impact it should have on our own vision of Church and parish.

But, alas, all too often these new visions and expectations have failed to materialise. In some places, parish life has continued undisturbed by the winds of change, while in others, genuine efforts have been made towards setting new goals, and constituting those structures necessary for their realisation. In particular, much energy has been expended on changing from what was primarily an authoritarian decision-making apparatus to one where co-responsibility and shared decision-making are all-important. At the parish level, the suggested structure for achieving this was the parish council.

Soon after the conclusion of the Second Vatican Council, many parishes set about constituting parish councils. The success of these councils was both mixed and uneven. Where they succeeded they usually had some concrete project in view such as the building or renovation of a church, a parish community centre, etc.. These councils occupied themselves largely with fund-raising and refurbishing the parish plant. Where no such refurbishing or renovation was needed, parish councils were often faced with a crisis of identity. What should they do? What was their precise function? As might be expected in these circumstances, they soon folded up, but not before they had experienced a lot of frustration, disillusionment and heartache. Not alone were these councils failing to unite the parish, they were frquently having the very opposite effect. A new pastor arriving in a parish was often advised to steer clear of resurrecting the parish council.

Much of the disappointment and disillusionment grew out of expecting too much too quickly. 'Priests expected the laity to understand their problems, to pick up the mantle of responsibility, to do more than talk, and certainly do more than grab the chequebook. People expected their priests to understand all their problems, to turn over everything to them, to do nothing without consultation and approval.'[1] But these goals and expectations were as far-fetched as they were unreal. Parish councils, as envisaged by the Second Vatican Council, did not materialise in the way intended by the Council Fathers.

With a view to resolving the present impasse, the 1983 *Code of Canon Law* has very rightly underscored the *pastoral* nature and function of these councils. It refers to them as 'parish pastoral councils'.(cf. C.536). Strictly speaking, there are no such things as 'parish councils' according to the Code, only 'parish pastoral councils' and 'parish finance committees' (cf. Cs. 536-537).

In September 1986 the Irish Catholics Bishops' Conference held a special five-day meeting at the Emmaus Retreat Centre near Dublin. The Bishops were guided in their deliberations by Cardinal Carlo Martini, Archbishop of Milan. At the end of the meeting Bishop Joseph Cassidy of Tuam, spokesman for the hierarchy, in a press release, gave a resumé of what had transpired during the meeting:

> Essentially the meeting was week of prayer and reflection on the mission of the Church, concentrating on two themes: the vocation and mission of the laity and, secondly, the working of the Bishops' Conference. Its purpose was not to produce precise formulae or a set of specific decisions but to identify areas of significance, to be followed by further consultation and discussion before decisions are taken.

As might be expected one of the areas targetted for special attention was the parish. The Bishops 'devoted a lot of time to thinking about the renewal of parish life, the building of community, greater participation by lay people in the life of the Church and at parish level.' They proceeded to identify certain structures which they would like to see in place in every parish throughout the country. One such structure was the parish pastoral council. That was September 1986. The following October the Synod of Bishops meeting Rome took as its topic *The Vocation and Mission of the Laity in the Church and in the World Twenty Years after the Second Vatican Council.* Pope John Paul II brought together these deliberations and discussions in his apostolic exhortation *The Vocation and Mission of the Laity*, published in December 1988.

Meanwhile the work of establishing parish pastoral councils, and the other structures that the Bishops had called for at their Emmaus Conference, was meeting with mixed success. Genuine attempts were being made to establish pastoral councils and to breathe new life and a pastoral way of thinking into existing, and sometimes struggling, parish councils. The task was difficult and painful. Some reported a greater level of success than others. But the one thing that all had in common was a crippling and debilitating uncertainty as to what precisely a parish pastoral council is, what it does and how it functions.

In this short book I hope to outline the nature, function and workings of a pastoral council. At this stage I feel that what G. K. Chesterton said of Christianity might well be applicable to our experience of pastoral councils to date: 'It is not that they have been tried and found wanting; they have have been found difficult and left untried.' Hopefully, this book will go some way towards overcoming that difficulty and inspire others at least to try them.

1. F.J. Rodimer, 'The Work of the Parish Council' in *Parish Leadership Today*, XXIIIrd Publications, 1979, p 52.

1. The Theological Foundations

Neither the Second Vatican Council nor the *Code of Canon Law* directly mandate the establishment of Parish Pastoral Councils. However, such councils are the inescapable consequence of the conciliar ecclesiology that is now firmly enshrined in the *Code of Canon Law.*[2]

For example, with regard to parish pastoral ministry, in both conciliar and postconciliar documents, the bottom line emerging is that priests do not exercise this ministry single-handedly. Not only are they not expected to do so, but they are positively discouraged from doing so. In the *Dogmatic Constitution on the Church*, n. 30, priests are reminded:

> [...] that they themselves were not established by Christ to undertake alone the whole salvific mission of the Church to the world, but that it is their exalted office to be shepherds of the faithful and also recognise the latter's contribution and charisms, that everyone will in his own way, with one mind, cooperate in the common task.[3]

But what is even more interesting is the manner in which the Council Fathers articulate the relationship of trust and collaboration that should exist between priests and their flock. In no. 37, they are remarkably unambiguous and forthright:

> [...] pastors indeed should recognise and promote the dignity and responsibility of the laity in the Church. They should willingly use their prudent advice and confidently assign duties to them in the service of the Church, leaving them freedom and scope for acting. Indeed, they should give them courage to undertake works on their own initiative. They should, with paternal love, consider attentively in Christ initial moves, suggestions and desires proposed by the laity.[4]

One might be forgiven for relegating to the realm of pious aspiration these theological niceties and lofty ideals, but for the fact that the same Council calls for the establishing of some institutions or agencies through which these ideals might be realised.

The *Decree on the Apostolate of the Laity*, of 1965, took these lofty ideals a step nearer to realisation. This Decree called for the setting up of 'councils to assist in the apostolic work of the Church' and *not* 'to assist in the apostolic work of the bishop'. Because of its pivotal role in our whole discussion, it is good to cite the relevant section of the Decree (n. 26):

> In dioceses, as far as possible, councils should be set up to assist the Church's apostolic work, whether in the field of evangelisation and sanctification or in the fields of charity, social relations and the rest; the clergy and religious working with the laity in whatever way proves satisfactory. These councils can take care of the mutual coordinating of the various lay associations and undertakings, the autonomy and particular nature of each remaining untouched.[5]

In response to this new vision, parish councils were established in many parishes in the aftermath of the Second Vatican Council, but they soon either disintegrated in accumulated frustration or devolved into finance committees. The one thing they were *not* was pastoral councils. The new *Code of Canon Law* deliberately adds the word 'pastoral' when discussing such councils.

That these councils mostly failed was probably due to the time needed for the new way of thinking, called for by the Council, to percolate into the minds and hearts of both clergy and laity alike. With the wisdom of hindsight and experience, we must now try to ensure that the same mistakes are not made all over again.

Out of a total of 1752 canons, the Code devotes but a single canon to this structure:

> C.536§1. If, after consulting the council of priests, the diocesan Bishop considers it opportune, a pastoral council is to be established in each parish. In this council, which is presided over by the parish priest, Christ's faithful, together with those who by virtue of their office are engaged in pastoral care in the parish, give their help in fostering pastoral action.

> §2. The pastoral council has only a consultative vote, and it is regulated by the norms laid down by the diocesan Bishop.

However, there are many other canons that shed light on how such a council should be organised and should function. I will refer to them later.

The Code also makes provision for diocesan pastoral councils (Cs.511-514), but it might be preferable to defer the establishing of diocesan councils until at least some of their parish counterparts are in place and operative.

Suggested further reading:

1. Vatican II, *Decree on the Apostolate of the Laity*, n. 10, (cf. Flannery, Vol. 1, pp 777-778.
2. *The Vocation and Mission of the Laity*, nn. 18-19, pp 46-51.
3. *Partnership in Parish,* Chpt 1, pp 3-10.

Footnotes:

2. The Code of Canon Law, Collins, London, 1983
3. A Flannery (Ed), Vatican Council II, *Conciliar and Post-Conciliar Documents*, Vol. I, Dominican Publications, Dublin, 1975, p 388.
4. Ibid., p 395.
5. Ibid., p 791.

2. *Parish Today: Vision & Reality*

The very idea of a parish pastoral council presupposes a certain vision of the parish. You shouldn't even contemplate establishing a parish pastoral council until you have clarified your own vision of the parish. Otherwise you run the risk of reverse logic – setting up a council and then wondering what to do with it! I would suggest that this has been the experience of many a parish council in the past.

At the beginning of his book, *Partnership in Parish*, Enda Lyons sets himself the task of defining and clarifying what parish means. I intend pursuing a similar course but by a different road.

The Parish as Territory

The notion of parish in the postconciliar Church has been radically overhauled. In the 1917 Code, a parish was essentially a territorial division of ecclesiastical property entrusted to a parish priest as a benefice or endowment. The pastoral care of souls was a responsibility flowing from the benefice. In return for looking after their pastoral needs, the parish priest enjoyed the fruits deriving from the benefice as his source of income. There were good benefices and bad ones.

In order to be promoted to a benefice, priests had to sit a kind of civil service exam called a *concursus*. A parish priest could only be transferred to an equal or a better benefice; otherwise his rights would be damaged. And a parish priest could not hold more than one parish because each parish was a benefice and holding more than one benefice was a scandal. Stole fees belonged to the parish priest, irrespective of who performed the sacred function.

The rights of the people of God whom he served did not count! People were very much secondary; parish boundaries were all-important. Indeed, it probably would not be an exaggeration to say that people were more important in death than in life!

According to Patrick J. Corish, Professor of History at Maynooth, competition between friars and diocesans to serve people was at its keenest in the cemetery. This was because the Council of Trent had entitled a parish priest to a fee if his parishioner was buried elsewhere, especially in a monastic cemetery. Funerals therefore were the perfect recipe for unseemly incidents, disedifying and public clerical quarrels.[6]

All this serves to highlight the concept of parish from which the Church is endeavouring to distance itself.

The Parish as People

The Second Vatican Council has turned this upside down. The notion of parish is no longer linked to to benefice or territory but to people and ministry. Parish is a person-centred reality. Its sole purpose for existence is to provide pastoral care for people. This shift in emphasis underpins conciliar and post-conciliar teaching on parish.

Insofar as I have been able to discover, the Second Vatican Council did not at any stage of its deliberations address itself directly to the concept of parish. It provided neither a definition nor a succinct description of what a parish is. But that is not to say that it overlooked or bypassed this vital structure. Rather it is from among its discussion of the rights and duties of priests and lay people in the Church that we must search out its underlying notion of parish.

When speaking about the rights and duties of diocesan priests, the Council Fathers give priority to the good of souls and the pastoral care of people. Everything else is subordinated to this – the right of a priest to be appointed parish priest, the security of his tenure as parish priest, the establishing of new parishes and the amalgamation and suppression of existing ones etc.. In a word : 'the care of souls is the whole function of a parish priest'.[7] Hence, when it comes to assessing a priest's suitability for governing a parish, consideration should be given not only his learning and zeal for the apostolate but also to those other gifts and qualities which are necessary for the proper care of souls. The

1983 Code of Canon Law takes this matter a step further when it states that the criterion for appointment to the office of parish priest is not seniority or *concursus*, but suitability to exercise pastoral ministry in the particular parish in question (cf. Cs. 521§3; 524). It is this very same preoccupation, namely, the good of people and the pastoral care of souls that prompted the Council Fathers to call for greater flexibility in the movement and transfer of parish priests from parish to parish as well as their spontaneous resignation on account of advanced years or for some other grave reason (when they) are unable to perform their duties adequately and fruitfully.[8]

Definition of Parish

The 1983 Code of Canon Law gives canonical expression to this new way of thinking when it defines parish as:

> ...a certain community of Christ's faithful stably established within a particular Church, whose pastoral care, under the authority of the diocesan Bishop, is entrusted to a parish priest as its proper pastor (C. 515§1).

Parish and its various structures then are at the service of people and not *vice versa*. It is within the context of parish that Christ's faithful hear and answer their call to holiness (Mt 5:48) or as Pope John XXIII was wont to say: it is the 'village fountain' to which all have recourse in their thirst. It is within the confines of parish that people have their first experience of church because 'it is there that the Church is seen locally. In a certain sense it is the Church living in the midst of her sons and daughters.'[9] The parish then is the *locus* or venue where Christ's faithful exercise their rights and fulfill their obligations within the Church. For the first time an attempt has been made to list these basic or fundamental rights. The Church has never been found wanting when it came to enunciating obligations binding her members (one has only to recall the minute and detailed regulations pertaining to Lenten fast and abstinence or the intricate norms governing the hearing of confessions etc.) but has often been accused of prevaricating when it came to outlining their rights and freedoms. The conciliar *Declaration on Religious Liberty, Dignitatis Humanae*, gave a new thrust to the quest for a statement of fundamental rights within the Church. In what has been called a 'Bill of Rights and Freedoms' the 1983 Code of Canon Law enumerates eighteen such rights (cf. Cs. 208 - 223). Among them is the right to be nourished by the word of God and the sacraments of the Church; the right of the faithful to make their needs, especially their spiritual ones, and wishes known to their priests; the right to participate in building up God's kingdom on earth by promoting and supporting apostolic action even on their own initiative. Now if individual members of the faithful enjoy such rights, somebody or some agency has a corresponding obligation to create the proper environment within which these rights and freedoms can be cherished and realised. According to the mind of the Church that person or agency is not the parish priest but the parish as such because 'the parish is the Church placed in the neighbourhoods of humanity.'[10] Indeed, it within this very perspective that the pope locates his discussion on parish:

> The ecclesial community, while always having a universal dimension, finds its most immediate and visible expression in the parish. It is there that the Church is seen locally. In a certain sense it is the Church living in the midst of the homes of her sons and daughters.
>
> It is necessary that in the light of the faith all rediscover the true meaning of the parish, that is, the place where the very 'mystery' of the Church is present and at work, even if at times it is lacking persons and means, even if at other times it might be scattered over vast territories and almost not be found in crowded and chaotic modern sections of cities. The parish is not principally a structure, a territory, or a building, but rather, 'the family of God, a fellowship afire with a unifying spirit', 'a familial and welcoming home', the 'community of the faithful'. At the beginning of his pontificate, Paul VI addressed the Roman clergy in these words: 'We believe simply that this old and

> venerable structure of the parish has an indispensable mission of great contemporary importance: to create the basic community of the Christian people; to initiate and gather the people in the accustomed expression of liturgical life; to conserve and renew the faith of the people of today; to serve as the school for teaching the salvific message of Christ; to put solidarity in practice and work the humble charity of good and brotherly works.[11]

Unlike other structures the parish has emerged from a period of transition and change with an enlarged stature and higher profile. In a very real sense the parish holds the key to the future of the Church. It is the power-house upon which the universal church depends. It is in the context of the parish that the vast majority of Christians pursue their vocation and work out their salvation. There the seeds of faith are sown and come to fruition. If people are to discover Christ, they will do so not through any private revelations of their own but in the midst of a faith-full and sustaining parish. For as St. Gregory the Great tells us: 'In the Holy Church all are nourished by each one and each one is nourished by all'. No effort therefore should be spared when it comes to building up a faith-full and vibrant parish.

Styles of Parish

People are often critical and even confused by the parish as they experience it. In the past people tended to know only one parish – the one in which they were born, brought up and settled down in. Parish priests moved parishes occasionally but this was more the exception than the rule. It wasn't unknown or unusual to have the same parish priest for thirty years or even longer. Today people tend to be more mobile and migrate from place to place for work opportunities or other reasons. Needless to say their experience of parish varies greatly. Being exposed to different styles of parish they are in a better position to evaluate what is happening in their own. In addition they bring with them hopes and aspirations and with little encouragement are happy to articulate them.

Every parish is in a certain sense unique, since it is not merely a sociological phenomenon but rather a faith-reality. Nevertheless, parishes tend to follow certain fixed patterns depending upon the priorities that the particular parish sets itself. In 1974 the Jesuit theologian, Avery Dulles, in his well known book *Models of the Church,* outlined different ways of perceiving the Church in terms of models or images. He identified five such models – none of which ever exist in its pure and exact form. In any given parish or ecclesial body different ingredients of these models will be readily identifiable,with one or other dominating. The reason for this is because the Church itself is a complex reality. No single model can ever exhaust its inner reality. Nor must they be seen in competition with one another. 'They should be made to interpenetrate and mutually qualify one another. None, therefore, should be interpreted in an exclusivistic sense, so as to negate what the other approved models have to teach us.'[12]

These same models - the major ones at least - can be applied equally well to the parish. Indeed, their application to parish will help in no small way identify the vision of parish out of which one is currently working. This is essential if one is to proceed towards a new vision of parish.

In order not to complicate things unduly, I shall limit my observations to three different styles of parish, one or other of which I feel is representative of the vast majority of our parishes.

1. Traditional Style

This style of parish operates out of the *institutional* model of Church. It places a high premium on visible, external structures and organisational elements. It perceives these structures to be the guardians and custodians of the Christian heritage. There is a clear distinction between the clergy and laity. The clergy are the benefactors or officers, mediating wisdom, knowledge and holiness to the laity. They are installed in this position of authority and prominence in and through the sacrament of orders. How often for instance have we heard people speak with respect and awe of the 'anointed hands of the priest'!

It is in the celebration of the parish liturgy that the particular model being invoked or subscribed to emerges with greatest clarity. In the traditional style parish the liturgy is something which is primarily done by the clergy for the people. The clergy mediate God's grace through a set series of ritual actions called the seven sacraments. Fidelity to liturgical regulations is of paramount importance. Active participation by the people is neither encouraged nor promoted. In this way of thinking the criteria for good liturgy is not its ability to create a sense of the holy in the worshippers but rather its clinical perfection and fidelity to the rubrics. In this rather empirical view of liturgy great emphasis is placed on what is statistically measurable. The spiritual life of the parish is gauged in terms of the number of baptisms, confirmations, confessions, communion, converts each year etc.. This is because the sacraments are deemed to be signals or signposts keeping people on the straight and narrow path leading to salvation. There is strong emphasis on what theologians call the automatic or *ex opere operato* effect of the sacraments i.e. the sacraments confer grace irrespective of the faith-disposition of the minister or recipient. God's word and those areas of parish life which are its direct corollaries such as adult religious education, preparation for the sacraments, Sunday liturgy, and youth ministry are all perceived to be of lesser importance. In a word such parishes tend to be over sacramentalised and under evangelised. All energy is directed at maintaining the *status quo.* Special ministers of the eucharist and readers are seen as good investment helping to keep the parish ticking over in the event of the clergy being unavailable or indisposed. Their role is perceived as one of maintenance in a time of declining religious vocations rather than as the exercise of a ministry which belongs to them by virtue of their baptism and confirmation. On the part of some parishioners there is a reluctance to accept special ministers of the eucharist or lay people as lectors. After all the priest has spent six or seven years preparing for this ministry and has been specially commissioned for it through the grace of ordination. They see the priest as a kind of general spiritual practitioner and want him to 'be all thing to all men'. They do not want a 'second fiddle' lector or eucharistic minister giving them Holy Communion or bringing it to them in their homes or in hospital. They want the man who was ordained to be available at their beck and call. Ultimately he is the only one who can consecrate the eucharist, forgive sins and administer the sacrament of the sick.

The strength of this style of parish is that it provides people with a strong sense of security and a sense of being in touch with the good old days. It gives a sense of stability in an ever changing world. It cushions people against the uncertainties thrown up by cultural and social change . The task of theology in this view is to defend the deposit of faith as handed down by the Teaching Office of the Church. There is a hankering after defined truths and moral absolutes. What one might call open or disputed questions in the area of doctrine or morals are kept to a minimum. Religion in general has more to do with the head than with the heart. Underlying all this is the tacit assumption that if people know the truth, they will somehow do it.

This style of parish is not without its limitations. It tends to be rather non-reflective and hierarchical. All power is mediated from the top with those lower down sharing in this clerical power. Various parish committees, if they do exist, fulfill little purpose other than rubber-stamping and affixing their signatures to what the parish priest has already decided. Consultation in the true sense of the word does not exist, except perhaps at a very superficial level and then only with regard to trivial issues. In the liturgy there is the risk of focusing on relatively unimportant aspects such as genuflections and incense etc. rather than its overall quality and authenticity. Little thought or effort is given to creating a spirit of togetherness and community which the Sunday liturgy might celebrate, confirm and deepen. Maintenance of the parish, both physically and spiritually, takes precedence over finding new ways to stimulate personal and communal conversion to the gospel.

The advantages of this style of parish is that it serves the deep needs of many people. Many are indeed happy to adopt a passive role when it comes to religion and Church. They are happy to 'pay, pray and obey'. It also finds a strong endorsement in official Church documents. The ecclesiology upon which it rests is alive and well in both conciliar and postconciliar documents. Pope John Paul's apostolic exhortation on *The Vocation and Mission of the Laity* endeavours to integrate this and other ecclesiologies. However, it is not the only ecclesiology found there nor indeed the most prevalent one.

2. Charismatic Style

On the other side of the spectrum is what one might call the *charismatic* type of parish. It revolves very much around the personality of the priest. It tends to be prophetic and is all the time searching out new ways of bringing the gospel to people. New initiatives and spontaneity are part and parcel of parish life. New pastoral projects are embarked upon. Some succeed, some don't but the important thing is that have at least been tried. This type of parish is likely to have an active Justice and Peace Committee concerning itself with local issues. The needs of the sick and elderly in the parish are catered for by concerned and dedicated parishioners, as indeed the needs of all other groups within the parish as well. In short the need of one is the concern or ministry of another. It is a parish where all are ministers. The parish is alive. Things are happening. There is more to parish life than the routine things of celebrating Mass, dispensing the sacraments and burying the dead. People feel involved. They sense that they are the parish. They look to their priests for leadership and inspiration and see them as specialists in the skills of ministry. Within the parish community they have certain duties 'especially entrusted' to them rather than 'reserved' to them (cf. C. 530). If for any reason the priest is has to be absent from the parish for a short period, parish life will continue powered by its own momentum. Those involved in the area of liturgical ministry will feel competent and confident enough to put on an appropriate liturgy even in the absence of an ordained minister.

Prayer will be an integral part of parish life, with all different forms and tastes being catered for i.e. from charismatic to Taizé, to the traditional Rosary and Benediction. In the liturgy itself creativity, spontaneity and experimentation will tend to override structure and rubrics. Great effort is put into the preparation and celebration of the Sunday liturgy with different individuals or families taking responsibility for organising certain parts it. The Sunday liturgy is such that it generates a sense of community or perhaps more accurately celebrates the faith-life and charity of the parish community. People attend Sunday Mass not out of a sense of obligation or under pain of sin but rather because they want to be there. The quality of the liturgical celebration is such that it attracts people from neighbouring parishes. Outsiders and newcomers to the parish will be impressed by the welcome they receive and the sense of loyalty that people have to their parish. This style of parish appeals to the more 'liberated' who wants to be actively involved in parish life.

The chief weakness of this style of parish is that it tends to revolve around the gifted personality of the priest, and might well rise or fall with his transfer. It will be unlikely that the priest who takes over will exude the same charisma. A caring parish spirit which has taken much time, tears and sweat to build can unfortunately be sacrificed or dismantled within a matter of months. A second weakness in this style of parish is that it can tend to be somewhat judgmental in character. One has to belong to it to be 'in' and to be saved and if one is 'out', one is very far out. From an ecclesiological point of view it runs the risk of being elitist.

Objectively speaking the ecclesiological threads running through this style of parish and animating it, are a mixture of those models which Avery Dulles refers to as Mystical Communion, Sacrament, Herald and Servant.

3. Classic Style

A third style of parish that one is likely to come across might be described as a well ordered combination of the *institutional* and *charismatic* types of parish. The emphasis here is on structure and well-thought out procedures. Little is left to chance or to spontaneity. All parish structures bear a strong hierarchical mark, with wide use being made of delegation. There is no ambiguity as to the ultimate source of authority and where the buck stops. This parish is abuzz with committees of every kind, each having a clearly defined area of competence and working within those parameters. The system boasts of efficiency but runs the risk of being run like a company or business, where the parishioners are the principal shareholders. The liturgy is performed with clinical perfection with different people performing those roles that pertain to them in accordance with liturgical and canon law. It often lacks spirit and charisma and seldom evokes a sense of commitment that will transform into values. It sees the sacraments as the chief means through which people are made holy. They have a twofold purpose: they are both remedies against sin and a means for the promotion of personal, spiritual growth. There is, however, a reluctance to acknowledge that the Holy Spirit can be at work outside of and apart from these structured activities. This type of parish believes in testing all spirits and would feel somewhat uneasy with the teaching of *Lumen Gentium* on the the role of the Spirit in the community:

> It is not only through the sacraments and the ministrations of the Church that the Holy Spirit makes holy the People, leads them and enriches them with his virtues. Allotting his gifts according as he wills (cf. 1 Cor 12:11), he also distributes special graces among the faithful of every rank. By these gifts he makes them fit and ready to undertake various tasks and offices for the renewal and building up of the Church, as it is written,'the manifestation of the Spirit is given to everyone for profit' (1 Cor 12:7). Whether these charisms be very remarkable or more simple and widely diffused, they are to be received with thanksgiving and consolation since they are fitting and useful for the needs of the Church.[13]

This style of parish appeals to many in that it offers a neat and well-packaged system. It tends to stifle and kill the charismatic and prophetic type of person. There are too many channels and structures to be got through before his/her idea or dream can take flesh and anyway in the process it will probably be stripped of its original inspiration and dynamism. It allows for innovation while at the same time being protected by a well-defined delegation and structured system.

The strength of this style of parish is that the various structures are so firmly in place that they are not easily unhinged by the transfer of the priest responsible in the first instance for putting them there. Its weakness is that it tends to lack that spiritual vitality and flexibility necessary for responding to changing pastoral circumstances.

Needless to say no one parish is likely to be a perfect example of any of these styles described. It is more likely to be a combination of all three with one or other being the more dominant. The transition from one style to another can be traumatic if not painful. But we can take consolation in knowing that the style of parish that will suit everybody has yet to be found. Parish should challenge and disturb us rather than soothe and comfort us. William Bausch sums this up very well in his book, *Ministry: Traditions, Tensions, Transitions,* when he writes:

> There is a spiritual formation that forces us to remember that no parish, of whatever style, is designed to be a comfortable island of wall-to-wall safety. The parish is no place to come for a comfortable social life of those exciting activities and programmes that console our consciences (we are after all doing something). It is no place to cater to our sense of well-being. It should be more than that. The parish must be there to create space where we are face to face with our true pain, know our sinfulness and consequently our need for God's grace and mercy.[14]

Suggested further reading:

1. *The Vocation and Mission of the Laity,* n.26, pp70-73.
2. *Partnership in Parish,* Chpts 2&5, pp 11-17; 35-49.
3. *Minstry: Traditions; Tensions, Transitions,* Chpt 8, pp 119-129.

Footnotes:

6. Cf. *The Irish Catholic Experience: A Historical Survey*, Gill & Macmillan, Dublin, 1985, p 103.
7. Vatican II, *Decree on the Pastoral Office of Bishops in the Church, Christus Dominus*, n. 31, (cf. Flannery, vol. I. p. 583)
8. Ibid.
9. John Paul II, *The Vocation and Mission of the Laity*, n.26
10. Ibid. n. 27.
11. Ibid n. 26
12. A. Dulles, *Models of the Church*, Dublin: Gill & Macmillan, 1976, p. 29.
13. n. 12, (cf. Flannery, Vol 1, p 363.)
14. p 127.

3 . The Mission of the Parish

The parish exists not for itself but for the mission of Christ. Its sole purpose for existence is the continuation of the mission of Christ in its entirety in this small corner of the Lord's vineyard, i.e. his healing, his teaching and his ministry of prayer and intercession on behalf of his people. The uniqueness of parish consists in the uniqueness of its mission, i.e. the leading of people to salvation by helping them know the gospel and live it out in their lives. Anything that impedes or hinders this objective is alien to the notion of parish.

Building Community

The primary task of every parish it to build community or to create that environment in which the Spirit of the Lord lives. It is within the community as such that the risen Lord resides. It is within the community that we experience God's love because Christianity by its very nature is incarnational. In Christ God has pitched his tent among us so that he might transform and touch our lives. It is as members of a parish community that the vast majority of Christians experience this transforming influence and pursue their vocation to holiness. This is how the Lord has designed it should be. 'He (the Lord) has, however, willed to make men holy and save them, not as individuals without any bond or link between them, but rather to make them into a people who might acknowledge him and serve him in holiness.'[15] From the faith point of view a community is a parish only to the extent that it reflects the presence of the risen Lord in its care and concern for people. St Luke in his description of the the early Christian community paints an idyllic picture of what the parish should be:

> The whole group of believers were united, heart and soul; no one claimed for his own use anything that he had, as everything they owned was held in common ... None of their members was ever in want, as all those who owned land or houses would sell them, and bring the money from them, to present it to the apostles; it was then distributed to any members who might be in need (Acts 4:32; 34-35).

> These remained faithful to the teaching of the apostles, to the brotherhood, to the breaking of bread and to the prayers.... The faithful all lived together and owned everything in common: they sold their goods and possessions and shared out the proceeds among themselves according to what each one needed. They went as a body to the temple every day but met in their houses for the breaking of bread; they shared their food gladly and generously; they praised God and were looked up to by everyone. Day by day the Lord added to their community those destined to be saved (Acts 2: 42; 44-47).

It is good at least to be aware of the ideal, even if there is little hope of ever achieving it. Ideals have a life and reality all of their own. They beckon us on to achieve greater things – feats that we had never even thought lay within our reach or compass. They set standards which we try to live up to, and provide us with norms against which we can measure our own performance. When we fail to live up to our ideals we tend to do one of two things. Either we change our lives or we change our ideals. The latter course of action is easy if we are ourselves the author of the ideals. But in the Christian perspective it is Christ himself who is the author. He has set the norms by his words and example. During the decades before they were written down in the Scriptures it was the apostolic community that kept these ideals and aspirations alive through preaching and teaching, exhortation and example. They have been handed down to us and form our Christian values. But the early Christian community of Acts must always be the ideal and model after which every parish strives. The knowledge that the ideal is rarely realisable should neither be a deterrent nor grounds for opting out.

Community a multi-level reality

Sociologists tell us that community admits of several different strata or tiers. It can exist at different levels. It is good to have a look at what each of these levels entail as our experience of parish often tends to reflect one or other of these. Seldom does it succeed in encapsulating all three simultaneously.

Community can be thrust upon people through their common experience of pain and suffering. It has often been said that the people of London never felt so united than when they were being bombarded nighly from the skies by enemy bombers during the Second World War. The remarkable response of the international community to the earthquakes in Armenia and Iran are perfect examples of community at this level. Traditional enemies bury their differences and come to the aid of a stricken people. Old feuds and opposing ideologies are forgotten and ignored for the time being at least. Hostilities are suspended. The very same is true at family level. It often takes a family tragedy or bereavement to bring together estranged members of the same family. Circumstances then have the capacity to bond people at a certain level at least.

Community can also exist at the level of ideas. Total strangers can find themselves at ease with one another when they discover that they share certain interests, beliefs or assumptions. The international political stage is a good example of this. Nations that share a particular political philosophy and ideology, even though separated culturally and geographically, tend to have much more in common than neighbouring states that espouse different philosophies. Any form of co-operation and working together tends to presuppose shared ideas, beliefs and assumptions between the partners.

Finally, community can exist at the level of action. Strikes and political demonstrations are perfect examples of this. The picket line can often bring together people who might have nothing in common otherwise. Over the past year in Eastern Europe we have witnessed different religious and ethnic groups uniting to topple oppressive political regimes and then suddenly discovering that they have precious little else in common. They lack any kind of bonding at the level of ideas or beliefs. Their sense of unity disintegrates and dies as soon as their primary objective has been achieved.

All too often it seems that Catholics are strong on community at the level of shared ideas and beliefs but weak at the other two levels. We tend to feel that Christian community begins and ends with the sharing of beliefs and doctrines or to put it more concretely with Sunday Mass. We have elaborate, credal formulas articulating what we believe but are weak when it comes to formulating an ongoing Christian plan of action. On the contrary we often spend much time and energy justifying our inaction e.g. failing to care for poor and marginalised in the parish.

A similar anomaly presents itself in the area of liturgy and ritual. The liturgy celebrates the justice of God as revealed by him in history, recorded in the Scriptures and proclaimed in the assembly of the faithful. But unfortunately our liturgy is usually little more than the celebration of common beliefs and seldom seen as a summons to action. Those who do not subscribe fully to those beliefs are denied full participation in the liturgy while those who perpetrate injustice and even violence encounter no such bar. Surely there is something amiss here.

This anomaly or contradiction becomes even more apparent at the level of personal spirituality. If I go the confession neither having asked forgiveness nor intending to be reconciled with others, isn't my symbolic action something of a contradiction? Or if I go the communion and ignore the plight of the poor and destitute of our world, isn't my ritual gesture somewhat empty and ineffective? Our beliefs and our convictions must be authenticated by our actions. Doesn't the Lord himself remind us that on Judgment Day it is actions that will count, not beliefs or convictions (cf. Mt 26: 31-46). 'It is not those who say to me, "Lord, Lord", who will enter the kingdom of heaven, but the person who does the will of my Father in heaven.' (Mt 7:21)

It is only when we interact with one another at all three levels that we can truly call ourselves a community. When our motivation for doing so is Christ-inspired rather than humanitarian, then we can boast of being a Christian community. The early Christian community that St Luke describes for us in the Acts of the Apostles combines community at all three levels. The disciples experienced themselves as a community under siege, taking refuge in that upper room for fear of the Jews (Jn 20:19). They were united at the level of faith and ritual (Acts 2:42) and at the level of action on behalf of a brother in need (Acts 4:34-35). Ideally this is the kind of community that every parish should be aspiring to. But reality all too often falls short of the ideal. In fact they rarely coincide. The process through which this gap is bridged is called evangelisation. The National Conference of Catholic Bishops of the United States, in its 1980 statement on *The Parish* gives a comprehensive and at the same time a simple decription of the term 'evangelization' – a term which confuses, if not frightens many people:

> This means not only calling active believers to ever deeper faith, but also bringing the message of Christ to alienated Catholics, inviting people to join in the Church's belief and worship, and making the gospel real by applying it to the issues and conditions of our lives. The witness to the gospel of Jesus acquires power from the continual reflection on faith and its demands to which parishioners devote themselves. Although parish undertakes special efforts to bring the gospel of Christ to those not active in the church community, it realises that the most effective instrument of evangelization is the parish's visible hospitality, its vitality, and its own faithfulness to Christ.[16]

Specific areas of evangelisation

1. Prayer

When Cardinal Martini arrived in Milan as its new archbishop he found a vast, sprawling industrial complex of some five million Catholics. He wondered what was the first chord he should strike in this enormous, industrial complex. He decided to put emphasis on prayer, silence and contemplation. The cynics wrote him off as being a scholar and academic but naive as far as pastoral reality was concerned. He proved them wrong. Much to his surprise the cathedral in Milan was regularly packed with young people anxious to hear the word of God, to listen to it, to contemplate it and pray about it. So many came came that they had to be dispersed into ten or twelve churches throughout the city. This little anecdote proves that prayer and the human spirit are inseparable.

Every parish must have prayer as a priority. It must encourage and facilitate group prayer whenever possible because wherever two or three are gathered together in the Lord's name he is there in their midst. (cf. Mt 18:20) The Church in recent years has been witnessing a mushrooming of prayer groups charismatic, Taizé etc. Some parishes have branches of the St Joseph's Young Priests Society, whose principal aim is prayer for vocations. Others have extended exposition of the Blessed Sacrament. What is certain is that no parish can survive without prayer.

2 Christian Formation

The Irish Bishops Conference, meeting at the Emmaus Retreat Centre in September 1986, expressed the wish that 'every parish in the country take repsonsibility for adult religious formation, either on its own, or in collaboration with neighbouring parishes.' These sentiments very much confirm the view of Pope Paul VI when he says :

> ...witness, no matter how excellent, will ultimately prove ineffective, unless its meaning is clarified and corroborated ... The good news proclaimed by witness of life sooner or later has to be proclaimed by the word of life. There is no true evangelisation if the name, the teaching, the life, the promises, the kingdom and the mystery of Jesus of Nazareth, the Son of God, are not proclaimed.[17]

Over the past decade Adult Religious Education Courses have been running successfully at different centres in each diocese throughout the country. Many people have participated in such courses but still they only constitute a drop in the ocean when compared to our Catholic and church-going population. The time has now come for each parish, or group of parishes, to be a centre of Christian formation and education. We are dealing with a highly educated and more sophisticated laity whose level of religious education has failed to keep pace with their other other accomplishments. Besides, the whole area of science, technology and politics are throwing up new issues and questions, all of which have at their core a religious dimension. Invitro-fertilisation, divorce legislation and the many questions pertaining to justice in our society are matters that defy simplistic solutions, deriving from an immature grasp of the Christian faith.

Other issues that must be faced is the renewed interest among Catholics of the word of God. Recent years have witnessed a growing hunger among lay people for the word of God. The parish should be in the forefront in catering for this hunger. Concerned about the number of young people getting sucked into different religious cults and sects the Catholic Bishops of the Province of Tuam warned against the risk of a literalist and fundamentalist approach to the Scriptures. Surely the best way to prevent people from being nourished on such a diet is by providing an alternative! Such an alternative need not necessarily be elaborate. It might begin rather modestly by reflecting on the Sunday readings and gradually progress to a study of the individual gospels as they occur in the three year liturgical cycle. No priest should feel overwhelmed or intimidated by this task. After all every priest has during his seminary days studied the Scriptures for several years. The surgeon to whose scalpel we submit ourselves on the operating table has completed a course of training of only roughly the same duration as the average priest. Like the surgeon the priest in his parish can call on the assistance of competent lay people who have already completed several courses in relgious education, not to mention other qualified people such as teachers and religious etc. Finally, there is no dearth of suitable reading and video material in this whole area right now.

3. Liturgical Celebration
In the same Emmaus document the Irish Bishops called for the establishing of a liturgy group in every parish in the country to assist the priest in the preparation of the Sunday Eucharist. This call no doubt is based on the twofold realisation that good liturgy simply does not happen – it has to be prepared, and that the liturgy is a community celebration, requiring full, active and conscious participation by all concerned.

In the mind of the Church the liturgy acts as a kind of spiritual barometer. It accurately reflects the faith and holiness of those celebrating it. If its execution is shabby, dull and uninspiring, isn't it because the community celebrating it is itself broken, fragmented and wounded! This is because the liturgy is primarily a celebration of what we are as a community. If there is no sense of unity or community among the people in the parish before they come to the Sunday eucharist, it is difficult to see how this can be created through the liturgy. Ideally, therefore, preparation for the Sunday liturgy begins not on Friday or Saturday but on Monday. It begins with building up a sense of community by promoting Christian ideals and the living out of shared values so that when the community assembles on Sunday, it truly has something to celebrate.

Preparation of the liturgy includes preparing both the environment where it will be celebrated and the people who will be celebrating it. Since the language of the liturgy is not confined to mere words but extends to symbols and gestures, careful consideration should be given to these also. After the assembly itself, the primary liturgical symbols are the altar, the ambo and the the president's chair. They should be the best the community can provide, exhibiting honesty and authenticity with regard to materials and craftmanship. They should harmonise with with one another and the whole liturgical environment. They should be arranged in such a such a way as to promote and encourage 'full, conscious and active participation in liturgical celebrations which is demanded by the very nature of the liturgy.'[18] The skills of artists and artisans in the parish might be utilised to bring out the diversity of liturgical themes and seasons.

But by far the most demanding and energy-consuming task is the preparation of the ministers taking an active part in the Sunday Eucharist. Most parishes now have a rota of readers and special ministers of the eucharist. These need initial training and continuing formation. The proclamation of the Lord's word is a new challenge each time, no matter how skilled or proficient the reader may be. The readings need to be prepared, prayed over and assimilated by the reader if they are to be a genuine source of spiritual nourishment to the hearer. Otherwise the word remains unbroken and the People of God undernourished.

Likewise special ministers of the eucharist, altar boys and those involved in the musical ministry need to be helped and motivated. The priest himself cannot possibly fulfill all of these tasks himself. If the liturgy is to be celebrated as the Church wishes it to be, the priest must mobilize the laity to assist him both in its execution and preparation. He cannot be a solo-runner in this area. He needs the assistance of a parish liturgy group.

4. Pre-Sacramental Catechesis

Another area targeted for special attention by the Irish Bishops is the whole area of pre-sacramental preparation for parents. In their Emmaus document they state that they 'would like to see in every parish in the country pre-sacramental preparation for all parents, for baptism; first confession; holy communion and confirmation.' This is in line with the 1983 Code of Canon Law which now for the first time makes such preparation mandatory. The reason for this is a new and enriched appreciation of the sacraments. They are primarily 'sacraments of faith' which in the words of the Second Vatican Council '... not only presuppose faith, but by words and objects (they) also nourish, strengthen, and express it.'[19] They do not dialogue with people who have no faith and are intelligible only within the context of faith. Pope Paul VI underscores the need for pre-sacramental catechesis when he states: 'to administer the sacraments without any firm basis of catechesis on the sacraments themselves, or of general catechesis, is to stultify their purpose and to a great extent deprive them of their efficacy.'[20] Several different programmes are available for each of the different sacraments. Once again the priest cannot himself be the architect fashioning each of these programmes. At most all he can be expected to do is to animate, facilitate and enable them to take place. He has to call on the resources and expertise of lay people to assist him in this vital task.

With regard to marriage, great and heroic work is already being done by committed lay people in preparing people for marriage. The fact that this being done at deanery level or outside the parish does not exonerate it of its responsibilities. There is the whole area of spiritual and liturgical preparation which is best done with each couple as such. There is no reason why other married couples should not act as kind of 'sponsors' to another couple both before and after their marriage. Traces of this practice are to be found in several African cultures today. It helps to promote marital stability at a time when the very institution of marriage is under threat.

5. *Specialised Ministry*

Within every parish there are different groups of people needing special pastoral care as such – youth, the handicapped, the sick, the elderly, the widowed, the bereaved etc. It is the parish as such that has pastoral repsonsibility for all of these groups because no individual person, ordained or unordained, can be expected to have all the necessary gifts and skills for ministering to these people. Different people are gifted in different ways. What needs to be done is to unearth and tap the various gifts and enormous resources that lie hidden in every parish community as a whole.

6. *The Alienated*

Of increasing concern to every parish must be the growing number of its disaffected and alienated members. It is not a new phenomenon – it is as old as Christianity itself. Jesus placed special emphasis on seeking out the lost in his parables of the lost sheep, the lost drachma and the lost son. (cf. Lk 15)

The reasons for alienation are manifold. In some instances the official Church or its representatives may have failed them. But in most instances they have voluntarily severed all visible links with the official Church either because of their disenchantment or because the shallowness of their own faith is insufficient to sustain them in a secular environment that is more uninterested than hostile to faith. In order to reach out to such people the Church must seek constantly the right approach and suitable language. On the one hand this involves standing firmly on the side of truth and on the other using all of one's skills to help the estranged to come to see and accept this truth in his life. In practice this means helping them to come to a realisation of where they are at in their faith-journey and recognising that conversion is not something instantaneous but rather a slow and gradual process.

A suitably adapted RCIA Programme is used widely in many countries today for reaching out to baptised non-believers. Its principal merit is that it acknowledges the gradualness of conversion and does not rush people into sacraments before they are ready for them. This kind of programme places strong emphasis on moral and spiritual conversion rather than on mere intellectual grasp of the faith. The programme is parish based and is celebrated in and through the liturgy. It is a source of renewal, not just to those directly involved, but indeed to the whole parish.

The final area of parish life targetted by the Irish Bishops for attention was the establishing of parish or pastoral councils in every parish where they do not exist. As this is the primary concern of this book, I shall devote the remainder to it.

Suggested further reading

1. Joseph Martos, *The Catholic Sacraments, Message of the Sacraments*, vol. 1, Wilmington, Delaware: Michael Glazier, Inc., 1983, Chpt 6, pp 183-194.
2. Joseph M. Champlin, *The Marginal Catholic*, Notre Dame, Indiana: Ave Maria Press, 1989.
3. Paul VI, *Evangelisation in the Modern World, Evangelii Nuntiandi*, 8 December 1985, ns. 17-24; 40-48; 56; (cf. Flannery, Vol. II, pp 711-761.
4. Michael Paul Gallagher SJ, *Struggles of Faith*, Dublin, The Columba Press, 1990, pp 2-23, 61-78.
5. USCCB, *The Parish: A People, a Mission, a Structure,* Washington DC, 1980.

Footnotes

15. Vatican II, *Dogmatic Constitution on the Church, Lumen Gentium* n. 9, (cf. Flannery, Vol. I, p 359.)
16. n. 22, pp 11-12.
17. *Evangelisation in the Modern World, Evangelii Nuntiandi*, n. 22, (cf. Flannery, Vol. II, p 720.)
18. Vatican II, *The Constitution on the Sacrd Liturgy, Sacrosanctum Concilium*, n.14, (cf. Flannery Vol. I, p 7.)
19. Ibid. n. 59, p 20.
20. *Evangelisation in the Modern World, Evangelii nuntiandi*, n. 47, (cf. Flannery, Vol. II, p 731.)

4. What is a Parish Pastoral Council?

In attempting to define any entity, I find it helpful to begin by stating what that entity is not.

What a Parish Pastoral Council is not

The parish pastoral council is ***not a legislative body*** for issuing decrees or statutes that the parish priest must either sign or veto.

The parish pastoral council is ***not a grievance-airing forum***. It is not the place for different groups and individuals scoring points off each other and manipulating parish policy. It is not the place for the adult choir to criticise and denounce the recently constituted folk choir. Neither should it be the priest's primary vehicle for taking the pulse of the parish.

The parish pastoral council is ***not a board of directors of a non-profit-making organisation***, with the parishioners as the principal shareholders.

It is ***not a democratically elected governing body***, because the Church is not a democracy but a ***hierarchical communion***. Within its complex, visible structure, it harbours both monarchical and democratic elements.

It is ***not simply a talk-shop*** complying with the letter of the law and episcopal wishes.

What a Parish Pastoral Council is

The parish pastoral council is a representative body of the faithful, working in close collaboration with the priest(s) of the parish, with a view to furthering the mission of Christ and his Church in this corner of the Lord's vineyard. It is collegiality in action at parish level.

There are many who would like to limit collegiality to the papal/episcopal and episcopal/presbyter relationships. But we cannot be selective when it comes to essentials. Collegiality is a quality which permeates the whole Church and, as such, must be seen to percolate right down to the smallest units which can properly be called Church.

Another word to describe collegiality is 'partnership'. The parish today is not so much a ***place where*** but a ***people who:*** a people who come together to share their diverse God-given gifts and talents by putting them at the disposal of the whole community.[21]

William J. Rademacher and Marliss Rogers, in their recently published book, *The New Practical Guide for Parish Councils*, list seven essential features or characteristics which a parish pastoral council should possess:

1. A parish pastoral council is *prayerful*. Prayer and intercession were an integral part of the life and ministry of Jesus. No body or group can claim to be continuing his mission unless they themselves are people of prayer.
2. A parish pastoral council is *pastoral*. What is meant by pastoral will be explored in more detail later when the concerns of the parish pastoral council are examined. Here it suffices to say that the council endeavours to take as its model Christ, the Good Shepherd. (cf. Jn 10).
3. A parish pastoral council is *representative*. It is a representative body rather than a body of representatives. Members must not see themselves as representatives for particular neighbourhoods, age-groups or organisations, in the way that a public representative might see him/herself. On the contrary, each member should have the spiritual well-being of all the people of the parish at heart.
4. A parish pastoral council is *discerning*. The first task of the council is to discern the needs, the hopes and aspirations of this particular community. Having evaluated the needs, etc., the gift of discernment is called upon once again in deciding what is feasible and practicable in the circumstances.
5. A parish pastoral council is *prophetic*. It examines the life and values of this community in the light of gospel values. In particular it addresses itself to issues of justice, peace, reconciliation and practical love.
6. The parish pastoral council is *enabling*. It is the mechanism through which the gifts and talents of different people and groups within the parish are recognised and utilised for the good of the whole community. The council makes use of these God-given skills and talents, helping people to discover

and develop talents that they themselves perhaps never knew they possessed. In this way the whole parish is enriched.

7. The parish pastoral council is *collaborative*. The parish is not an isolated cell or unit. It exists within a diocese and is part of the Church worldwide. The pastoral council is concerned, not just with promoting the good of its own parish community, but has the interests of the diocese and, indeed, of the whole Church at heart. It is not parochial, therefore, in the pejorative sense of the word. It does not propose schemes or projects which are at variance with diocesan policy or conflicts with Church teaching and discipline.

Parish Pastoral Council v Finance Committee

A parish pastoral council always takes precedence over a parish finance committee. Both are integral parts of parish life; both are at the service of parish, but in different ways. Funds are indeed necessary in order that the parish should be able to pursue its mission and goal, but the parish exists primarily for the purpose of mediating pastoral care to its members. It is not not a fund-raising organisation. In fact the more a pastoral council can distance itself from money matters and maintenance the better, because it is not a finance council. We know from experience that money matters have the extraordinary knack of invading, dominating and even derailing the most sacrosanct of discussions. The best way of ensuring that this does not happen to the pastoral council is to have a totally separate finance committee. This is exactly what Church law proposes when it opts for total separation between pastoral and finance committees. 'In each parish there is to be a finance committee to help the parish priest in the administration of the goods of the parish.' (C. 537) Its structure, function and manner in which it conducts its business are very different from those of the pastoral council. Indeed, it might be preferable to first establish a finance committee, put it in place and only then set about constituting a pastoral council. This line of approach has the advantage of precluding any misunderstandings that either priests or people might have about the precise nature and role of the pastoral council when the time comes for establishing it.

> The finance council is a group of lay people who assist the pastor in the administration of the parish, preparing budgets, financial statements, making investments, overseeing property and facility management, fund-raising, church building and so on. The finance council does not make priorities or set policy. It is the pastoral council, in cooperation with the staff and pastor, that sets forth policy for the parish.[22]

The Concerns of a Parish Pastoral Council

By its very definition, the parish pastoral council must concern itself with pastoral matters, i.e. the whole range of pastoral activities within the average parish. How does one set about determining or specifying the different areas of pastoral activity with which this council should concern itself?

More than ever before, the law of the Church has spelled out in detail the pastoral activities of the priest. It does so in two rather lengthy canons, most of which are transcribed almost verbatim from the *Decree on the Ministry and Life of Priests.* It is good to list these particular areas, because they are also the concern of the parish pastoral council:

- proclaiming the word of God;
- celebrating the Eucharist and sacraments;
- instructing the faithful;
- educating the young in Christian values;
- promoting social justice;
- reaching out to the poor and elderly;
- comforting the sick and dying;
- leading people in prayer, especially in family prayer.
  (cf. Cs. 528-529).

Bertram Griffin provides us with a very comprehensive description of the council:

> The purpose of the pastoral planning council is to study the life and activity of the people of God; that is, to research the

> needs, the ideas, the hopes of the people of God, their actions and so on; secondly to evaluate the parish in conformity with the gospel; and, thirdly, to recommend policies, procedures and programmes. The job of the parish council therefore, is not to decide whether the American flag will be in or out of the sanctuary, or whether coleslaw will be served at the parish dinner. The job of the parish council is to deal with the mission of the Church, long-range and short-range goals and objectives, and to design those procedures and processes by which the pastoral work of the Church is accomplished.[23]

The following diagram might be useful in trying to envisage the range of concerns which might be represented on a typical pastoral council:

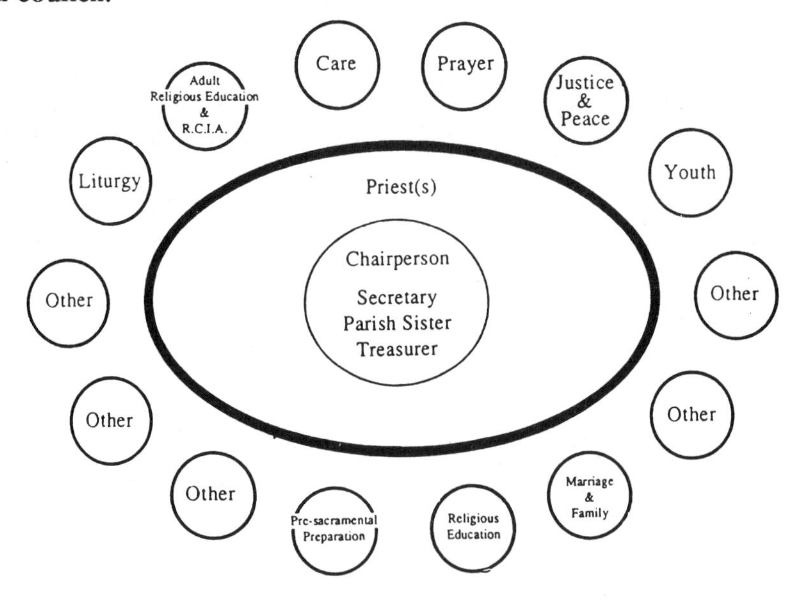

The different areas mentioned are areas for pastoral concern in the average parish. I have deliberately left some areas blank in the diagram, in order to cater for special pastoral problems at a given time or within a particular parish.

A particular parish may be made up predominately of retired people or young families or of flats. These factors obviously will have a bearing on the shaping of the pastoral council. So, the composition of the pastoral council may vary from parish to parish from one time to another. This is precisely because of what this council is.

> In a word, the role of the pastoral council is to help the pastor identify pastoral needs in the parish, help him plan pastoral programmes and improve pastoral services, evaluate the effectiveness of existing programmes and services with a view to their improvement or, at times, their substitution or termination. [24]

A cursory glance at the above diagram might very easily give the impression that pastoral councils are ideally suited to large, sprawling urban and suburban parishes. These parishes have the population density, the pastoral scope and are more likely to possess the necessary resources for a wide range of pastoral initiatives. Having an effective pastoral council in these circumstances makes a lot of sense. In a very real way it assists the priest in the full range of his pastoral ministry.

But what about a small rural parish, where the priest knows each parishoner personally and their family history for generations? Is a pastoral council necessary in such circumstances or is it superfluous? The most comprehensive answer to these questions is 'yes' and 'no'. Every parish community needs a parish pastoral council by virtue of what a parish is, but not every one needs as elaborate a pastoral council as the one outlined above. Pastoral needs and scope will vary from one parish to another and certainly from a rural to a city setting. If the parish is for people then the parish pastoral council should be tailored to the needs of the people in the particular parish in question.

One or more pastoral councils within a parish?

Finally, the question is often raised whether a parish, having separate and fairly autonomous communities, should have one overall pastoral council for the whole parish or one for each community? In light of what has already been said, one must put people before structures. A pastoral council can only function effectively within a community conscious of its own identity as a community of faith.

I would suggest therefore that each worshipping community – and it is worshipping together that ultimately builds and shapes a sense of identity – should have its own pastoral council responsible for pastoral planning and action within that particular community.

This should not constitute a threat to the overall unity of the parish – no more than the unity of a diocese is threatened by having pastoral councils in each parish.

At the end of the day, the decision to have one or more pastoral councils or groups within the parish should be determined on the basis of what will best serve the mission of the Church in this particular parish.

Suggested further reading:

1. *The Vocation and Mission of the Laity,* nn. 19-27;34;45-48. pp 48-76;95-99;135-143.
2. *Partnership in Parish,* Chpts 3&4, pp 18-34.
3. *The New Practical Guide for Parish Councils* , Chpts 4&7, pp 19-30; 87-97.

Footnotes:

21. Cf. Enda Lyons, *Partnership in Parish,* pp 68-71.
22. B. Griffin, "The Parish and Lay Ministry', in *Chicago Studies,* 23(1984), p 59.
23. Ibid., pp 58-59.
24. J. Keating, 'Consultation in the Parish', in *Origins,* 14(1984-1985), p 265.

5. *The Consultative Process*

Theological basis

Going to meetings, some claim, has become the modern form of penance in the Church. Some have been even bold enough to suggest that when the Parousia arrives Father will be at a meeting. But whether we like it or not meetings are an integral part of modern day living and are assuming an ever increasing role in ecclesiastical life since the Second Vatican Council. The higher one ascends the hierarchical ladder, the more meetings one is expected to attend. In ecclesiastical circles at least the reason for this is the importance that the postconciliar Church attaches to consultation. It is the standard way of arriving at decisions within the ecclesal community. The Synod of Bishops at universal level and the Council or Priests at diocesan level act as consultative bodies to the pope and bishop respectively. Within the parish structure the parish pastoral council and the parish finance committee are consultative to the parish priest. (Cs. 536§2 & 537) The consultative process itself rests upon a number of theological presuppositions, all of which are firmly rooted in conciliar teaching:

1. The fundamental equality of all believers: The Second Vatican Council underscored the fundamental equality of all believers. This equality is rooted in their baptismal dignity. Although there is an essential difference between the priesthood of the ordained and that of the baptised this translates into a difference of function rather than one of status. Book II of the 1983 Code of Canon Law is a perfect example of this. While the old Code began with the rights and duties of the higher ranking ecclesiastics, the present Code begins with the rights and duties of all Christ's faithful and gradually works it way down to the rights and duties specifically entrusted to the clergy.

2. The charismatic dimension of the Church: As we have already noted in chapter 2 above the Council Fathers drew attention to the role of the Spirit in the ecclesial community. His gifts are not in any way the preserve of the clergy but are distributed widely among all the People of God. His gifts of wisdom, knowledge, understanding and right judgement are assets that cannot be ignored when it comes to the exercise of ministry within the ecclesial community.

3. The Church is basically a 'communio'. Among the many strands of ecclesiology found in conciliar and post-conciliar teaching this is the predominant one. The Church is primarily a pilgrim people in communion with God and each other. Responsibility for mission is shared by all in the communion, although in different degrees depending on one's gifts and function within the 'communio'. This 'communio' finds expression in and through the functioning of consultative bodies. In them various charisms come into play in determining what is best for the Church in its given, pastoral circumstances.

Consultative v Deliberative

Today there is much discussion about 'consultative voice' and 'deliberative voice'. Both are equally valid ways of participating in decision-making, whether in the secular or religious sphere. The decision-making process is complex. It is primarily a process which involves the gathering of sufficient information, sifting through assembled data with a view to identifying the different possible options, selecting one or other of those options by an act of the will of the person or persons responsible for making the decision. In a decision-making body where the members enjoy a deliberative voice, each person has a say at all stages of the process, including the act of the will through which the decision comes into being. On the other hand if the body has a consultative voice only, its input is at all stages apart from the final one, namely: the act of the will through which the person or persons responsible actually make the decision.

In the Church the vast majority of structures or bodies are consultative but that is not to say that the superior may arbitrarily dismiss or ignore the advice on offer. Canon 127§2.2 of the Code of Canon Law warns against such misuse or abuse of the consultative process. When the law prescribes that a Superior requires the *advice* of certain persons in order to act validly, 'the Superior is not in any way bound to accept their vote, even if it is unanimous; nevertheless, without what is in his or her judgement, an overriding reason, the superior is not to act against their vote, especially if it is a unanimous one'. The *rationale* behind this of course is that decisions that cannot or will not be implemented are worthless. They are not worth the paper they are written on. Thus, if the decision of the Superior favours a certain course of action while that of his/her consultative body are unanimous in proposing an alternative, there is little point in the Superior proceeding with the act of the will through which the decision is made. If the decision of the Superior is at variance with the general consensus, it is very likely that the consultaive process has gotten bogged down somewhere along the way. In these circumstances the only solution would seem to be a levelling of the playing pitch and starting from scratch all over again. Indeed, one might do well to introduce a referee and perhaps even some substitutes in order to shed new light on the issue under consideration and isolate the difficulties. New blood can often inject new life and energy into a tired and ailing team. A good facilitator enables a group to realise its full potential.

Consultation: a search for Consensus

Consultative decision-making reaches decisions through consensus. In this process, the way in which the decision is arrived at is almost as important as the decision itself. Consensus shows respect for each person's point of view and contribution and carefully avoids dividing the group into opposing camps. Here there are no vested interests and no positions to be doggedly defended. All participants share the same objective, namely: the best solution to the issue currently being discussed. They see themselves as allies, searching for the truth. In this process each members feels that he/she exercises equal influence in shaping and determining the ultimate outcome. The fact that an individual's contribution may not be reflected in the final decision, does not necessarily mean that it did not have a bearing on that decision. Because of its inherent respect for the views of all, and its singlemindedness in its search for truth, consensus brings out and expresses more clearly the nature of the Church as a 'communion of each Christian with Christ and the communion of all Christians with one another.'[25]

Arriving at decisions through this process, however, demands a lot of time, patience, skill and discernment. Some of the skills required are: gathering the right kind of information; reading the signs of the times; helping people to vent their feelings and fears; giving people a sense of belonging to parish; listening patiently to their stories and giving them new hope and visions that will enable them to face the future with enthusiasm and courage.

The value of the consultative process is that it repects the entire life-cycle of the decision-making process. A decision, like a law, has a life all of its own. Within its life-cycle there are preordained stages:

- at one point it is conceived,
- at another it is born,
- then it lives,
- until it dies and is buried.

A decision is *conceived* when somebody wielding influence within the community perceives a value suitable and desirable for the community to embrace. In addition he/she feels the community is capable of realising it, eg. the provision of homes for the elderly. It goes through its gestation period when the data and information is being gathered and evaluated.

It is *born* when the person wielding authority within the community chooses a certain course of action and mandates that it be acted upon, eg. that a certain number of houses be build for the elderly.

Yet, no matter how good or laudible the decison may be, it has little life or significance in the real world until it begins to take shape. The decision begins *to live* when the architect's plans are translated into buildings.

Finally, all decisions have a life-span. When they no longer serve any useful purpose they *die* and are replaced by new decisions. In the Church people are often slow to make decisions because they fear the impact they may have on existing ones. When decisions no longer serve the good of the ecclesial community, they should be killed off and buried rather than be allowed to linger on to a slow and painful death. Structures that serve the Church well in one age don't necessarily do so *ad infinitum*. The decision, therefore, to terminate the life of certain structures is often as important as the decision to establish them in the first instance.

Robert Kennedy underscores the life-cycle of a decision by drawing our attention to the various steps involved in the consultative process. Decision-making is not to be equated with 'choice-making'.[26] Choice-making is only one stage of decision-making, and not necessarily the most important one. Kennedy identifies the following stages:

1. The Creative Idea Stage
In order to be able to choose at all, one must have at least two options available. If there is no alternative there is no choice. The more options there are the greater the quality of the choice. In the consultative process, therefore, there is room for the creative and imaginative type of person, perhaps even for the dreamer.

But visionaries and dreamers are not usually the type of people that we associate with good decision-making. In the consulative process this is simply not so. The beauty of this process is that it capitalises on the strengths of people. We are all familiar with the old cliché that 'a team is as strong as its weakest link'. But in the consultative process the opposite is the case. It utilizes the strengths of people. One person's strength in particular area compensates for another person's weakness in that same area and *vice versa*. A creative person is rarely a good choice-maker just as a good choice-maker need not necessarily be creative. When it comes to weighing up the feasibility and advantages of a particular course of action, the imaginative person is usually not the most realistic of judges or assessors. But it must be remembered that no such appraisal would have been necessary had it not been for the vision and inspiration of the imaginative person in the first instance.

2. The Fact-Finding Stage

To assess how realistic and realisable dreams and visions may be, one must be in possession of the factual data relevant to these particular circumstances. Facts are the raw material of good decision-making. Half-truths and conjecture lead invariably to bad decisions. The role of the fact-finder and the information-gatherer coincides more or less with that of the cross-examiner in the courtroom. The manner in which the fact-finder presents his information will exercise an enormous influence on the eventual choice.

In the human condition there tends to be an inherent propensity to assert as facts what one desires to be facts rather than what one has ascertained to be so. Not being prepared to put in the required investigative effort necessary in order to equip oneself with the necessary data and information often results in having recourse to hearsay or, worse still, to inventing the data required. The person who arrives at a meeting with no homework done is his/her own worst enemy. I'm convinced that the time spent at meetings could be halved, if the participants were to arrive equipped with the necessary data. Many unproductive, boring and frustrating hours of meeting could be avoided if the fact-finders had done their homework. This is all the more important if the meeting is primarily informational rather than decision-making as such.

Once again the fact-finder is a particular kind of person who has a searching and questioning mind. He leaves no stone unturned in his quest for the necessary information. Having gathered the information his/her next task is to assemble and present it to the choice-makers. The latter usually have no other information to go on other than that presented by the data people. Hence, they are really the most influential people in the whole decision-making process. Anyone interested in quality decisions can ill-afford to skip this vital stage in the process.

3. The Choice-Making Stage

Making the actual choice between the different options available is probably the easiest and least demanding step of all. The pros and cons of the different courses of action, insofar as they can be envisaged, are weighed up and evaluated. What appears to be the best option is chosen and the person or persons charged with making the decision give their assent to this particular course of action. The idea of voting at this stage is alien to the whole process. It undermines it completely, for it amounts to saying that all the time and energy already expended in searching out the best option were largely a waste of time. The person anxious to press for a vote feels that there are other more compelling areas or angles to the issue that haven't received sufficient consideration by the group. He/she has not yet been convinced by the arguments adduced in favour of the option chosen and, by voting, wishes to be disassociated from the final decision.

The making of the choice does not conclude the decision-making process. Indeed, it might well be said that it is little more than a statement of intent or a good intention. It has reached the stage of conception. But it still remains to be born into the real world, to grow and to mature.

4. The Implementation Stage

Everybody knows that decisions which cannot be implemented are bad decisions. It is a futile exercise to make decisions that will not be implemented. The priest, for instance, may wish to initiate a pre-baptism programme in his parish, but for this he needs the assistance and cooperation of a number of committed lay people. There are various pre-baptism programmes available, and of these the priest favours one while the people most likely to be implementing the programme favour another. While in theory the parish priest may insist on his own preference, in practice it would be unwise of him to do so.

5. The Evaluation Stage
This is a stage that is frequently neglected. One must always be open to modify and change one's course of action in the light of new circumstances. In the area of pastoral decision-making the old axiom holds true: ***salus animarum suprema lex*** (the salvation of souls is the highest law). Very few, if any, decisions are sacrosanct or immutable.

However, when evaluating projects and structures resulting from prior decisions, care must be taken to keep in mind the uniqueness of the Church's mission, the dignity of the person and the law of charity. Many might feel that the altar rails, or the stained glass windows, which make the church so stuffy and dark, should be removed from it now that it is being renovated. At a purely business level this might make a lot of sense, but at the religious and ecclesial level it might be counterproductive. Such a decision might in fact split the community down the middle and the whole purpose of the parish, namely the building of community, is then out the window.

Prerequisites for Consultation
James H. Provost, in an article in *The Jurist,* suggests a number of prerequisites if this process is to work. Most important of all is the attitude with which it is undertaken.[27] Like everything else, this process can be circumvented and end up being nothing more than consultation in name or a rubber-stamping operation. Condescension, paternalism and favouritism are the enemies of consultation. They eat into and destroy that openness, mutual trust, confidence and creative tension that should characterise this process. The priest can in fact do more harm than good by appointing to his consultative body people who are in awe of him and are intent on saying or doing only what pleases him. He is denying himself the right to proper consultation and defeating its very purpose.

For consultation to take place the body must assemble together collectively. A superior consulting with a group on a one-to-one basis is not what the Church understands by consulation. There has to be interaction and cross-fertilisation of ideas and points of view between all concerned.

The working of the consultative process demands a high degee of tolerance and flexibility on the part of its users. One has to be prepared for doing an about-turn with regard to one's views at any stage during the process. The reason for this is obvious – he/she may hiterto have been relying on inaccurate or inadequate information.

The consulative process demands commitment and work from all intent on using it. It stands or falls on the preparedness of people to do their homework in advance. When they come to the meeting they are then in a position to share views that have been thought about and reflected upon, and so are not condemned to speaking or listening to opinions that originate off the top of the head.

The final prerequisite is that consultation must be given a fair chance. Consultative bodies in the Church are very much in their infancy. They are still less than thirty years old. They are feeling their way and often groping in the dark. They are the subject of much scepticism, if not cynicism, from above and below. It is all a matter of striking the right balance. Rome wasn't built in a day.

When to use the consensus process

The consensus process is the one which best fits the nature of the Church. Given that it consumes so much time, commitment and energy, it should be used only when deliberating on significant issues of parish life. If it is overused, participants may begin to resent the demands being made on their time and may be less enthusiastic to invest the necessary time and energy when an important issue comes up for consideration. Finally, if the council is to have faith in itself and credibility in the parish at large, the priest, to whom it is advisory, should only for the gravest of reasons act contrary to the prevailing view of the group (cf. C.127§2.2.) Otherwise the message that the group may be getting is that their contribution is no more than window-dressing, i.e. supplying a veneer of consultation to what is basically a one-man decision.

Chairing a Parish Pastoral Council Meeting

Consensus should not be confused with simple agreement. Simple agreement lacks the ingredient of labouring together to reach that agreement. Neither should it be confused with large-majority decision, which smacks of voting procedures and implies that a small minority does not back the decision reached.

Arriving at decisions through the consultative process can be one of the most trying, wearisome and frustrating experiences a person will encounter. Yet it can be one of the most gratifying and fruitful.

The council aims at reaching a consensus by listening to and sharing the points of view of the different members. This style of decision-making can function only within a climate of openness, mutual trust and acceptance.

James F. Trent gives an excellent description of this type of decision-making:

> Consensus is not the same as unanimity. Rather, it is a state of affairs where communications have been sufficiently open, and the group climate has been sufficiently supportive, to make everyone in the group feel that they had a fair chance to influence the decision. Someone then tests for the 'sense of the meeting', carefully avoiding a formal procedure such as voting. If there is a clear alternative to which most members subscribe, and if those who oppose it feel that they have had a chance to exert influence, then a consensus exists. Operationally it would be defined by the fact that those members who would not take the majority alternative, nevertheless, understand it clearly and are prepared to support it.[28]

Consensus, therefore, is arrived at through an open and candid airing of views. The ability to listen is often more important than the ability to speak. The topic under consideration might be anything, e.g. establishing a youth ministry programme in the parish. There may be many and divergent views as to how this project might be approached. The individual, who holds strong views at variance with the majority view, is given the opportunity to explain his view fully and sway the majority to his way of thinking. However, if in the end he fails to do so, he should not feel aggrieved or ignored and should be glad to go along with the majority view.

The Chairperson

Obviously the skills required for this consensus-building process do not come easily. They have to be learned and acquired over a period of time. Much will depend on having the right chairperson.

The chairperson should be appointed on the basis of having the necessary skills to handle the consultative process effectively. The priest does not have to be chairperson. Where he is not, he becomes President of the council and presides at all meetings.

Process v Content

We cannot pay too much attention to the question of process. When suggestions at a meeting are met with silence, when getting volunteers is an uphill struggle, when there is a dearth of topics to discuss, then perhaps what needs to be examined is the process. Is the parish seen to be a one-man-show where discussion of the key issues is deliberately avoided or the opinion of the priest must always prevail? 'Content' and 'process' relate to each other like the two wheels of a bicycle. One is useless without the other. In the past, attention was devoted almost exclusively to content. Today there is the risk of the other extreme. The ideal is to work the proper balance between them both. Neither one can be sacrificed for the other.

Suggested further reading:

1. *Actions Speak Louder*, Chpts 4-7, pp 21-47.
2. *The New Practical Guide for Parish Councils,* Chpts 5&10, pp 31-58; 132-157.

Footnotes:

25. John Paul II: *The Vocation and Mission of the Laity*, n.19, p 49.
26. Cf. 'Shared Responsibility in Ecclesial Decision-Making', in *Studia Canonica*, 14(1980), p 8.
27. 'The Working together of Consultative Bodies – Great Expectations', in *The Jurist* 40 (1980), p 262.
28. 'Shared Decision Making', in *Parish Leadership Today*, p 60.

6. Setting Up a Parish Pastoral Council

Introduction

Do not rush into setting up parish pastoral councils without first completing the groundwork and readying the site. A pastoral council is something that should evolve into being rather than be created out of nothing. It is not for every parish because it demands a certain type of leadership. Bishop Michael Murphy, of Cork and Ross, articulates very well what will be required of the priest:

> A new style of leadership will be expected of the priest. This will be a participatory style, which involves: inviting people, promoting group discussion, listening, clarifying issues, identifying a lack of information, reminding the group of its agreed mandate. A sincerity of purpose, a respect for each person, an openness to new learning are personal qualities essential to this style of leadership [...]. It can be painful and troublesome in the adjustment of leadership styles.

There is an old Irish proverb which reads: *Tús maith leath na hoibre* (A good beginning is half the work.) There is also an old legal axiom which states: That which affects everybody should be approved by everybody. These two snippets of wisdom underscore the vital importance of laying the proper foundations before attempting to establish a pastoral council.

The successful launching of a pastoral council presupposes that all the priests of the parish are fully behind it and committed to it. Anything less than full and enthusiastic commitment from the clergy will render the project extremely difficult, if not futile. Parish pastoral councils are the concrete expression of 'partnership in parish'. If that spirit of partnership and cooperation is not evident among the priests of the parish, it is hard to expect it to permeate the priest-people relationship.

Membership

This is one of the thorniest issues of all. How does one get the right people to volunteer, to be elected, and to serve on a parish pastoral council? I believe that much will depend on the manner in which the council is explained and marketed. This will come up later when we talk about models for establishing parish pastoral councils.

In selecting or electing people to serve on a parish pastoral council, the manner in which the consultative process works merits serious consideration. People used to the managerial or trade union model for reaching decisions may indeed find it difficult to adjust to the consultative process. As members of a pastoral council, they may try to impose the voting model, which is alien to the consultative process. Voting demonstrates efficiency rather than effectiveness. There will almost always be winners and losers, and so it does not secure agreement and guarantee commitment. The attitude of the disgruntled loser will range from non-participation to active opposition. This is the very last thing that is needed in a parish pastoral council.

Again, the individual who is manifestly interested only in finance and administration might be a suitable candidate for the parish finance council but not for the pastoral council.

The most fundamental question, of course, is the person's interest in promoting the overall mission of the Church.

There are certain criteria and qualifications that should be kept in mind when selecting members:

Criteria for selecting/electing members of the pastoral council:

a) They should be interested in promoting the overall pastoral mission of the Church.

b) They should be capable of grasping the meaning of Church and its mission.

c) They should be believing and praying Christians.

d) They should be baptised members of the Catholic Church.

e) They should be willing to undertake a course of preparation and ongoing formation.

f) They should be willing to devote considerable time and effort to committee meetings etc..

g) They should be able to work with other people.

h) They should accept the teachings of the Second Vatican Council.

Since the function of the council is to advise the priest on the pastoral ministry of the Church, its members must make every effort to deepen their own knowledge of the Church and its mission, through study, prayer and recollection. Part of every meeting should be devoted to prayer and study. One of the greatest challenges facing every pastoral council will be the formation of its members. A failure to appreciate this has been one of the causes for parish councils floundering in the past.

Selection or Election?

I would be inclined to follow the model currently in use for the council of priests (cf. C.497). I would envisage some members being:

- *ex officio*, e.g. all the clergy of the parish and the parish sister (or pastoral assistant) if there is one;
- *nominated directly by the priest(s)*, people deemed to be an asset to a pastoral council because of their particular talents and skills or positions they already hold in the parish, e.g. youth minister;coordinator of readers and Eucharistic ministers, head of the St Vincent de Paul Conference, etc.
- *elected by the parishoners themselves* (these should number at least half of the entire council).

The membership of the pastoral council should probably be between fifteen and twenty persons. Anything more would be too unwieldy. Besides, experience tells us that committees that are too large seldom achieve their objectives. It is usually subcommittees that do the work and report back to the central committee.

In deciding the best number of members for the parish pastoral council, remember that any meeting will not have any more than about 75% of the members in attendance.

Models for Establishing a Parish Pastoral Council

There is no ready-made model suited to all parishes and circumstances. Ultimately it will be a matter for each parish to decide on which model, or combination of models, is best suited to its needs. A number of models have been used successfully in different parishes in Ireland:

a) The Parish Assembly Model

Neighbourhood Masses are arranged throughout the parish and are followed by a discussion on the pastoral needs of the parish. The priest airs the idea of a parish pastoral council and invites each neighbourhood to elect two or more people to represent them at a parish assembly to be held later. He also directs his Sunday homilies to this theme for a number of consecutive Sundays so as to reach those who cannot be present at neighbourhood Masses.

At the Parish Assembly, the whole notion of parish is further explored and discussed. A skilled facilitator provides the input and directs the day. Members are nominated and elected to form a parish pastoral group. Other members are nominated to this group by the priest(s) of the parish. They are all formally commissioned at a parish Liturgy to which the whole parish is invited. At the commissioning ceremony, the representatives commit themselves to undertaking the course of preparation and ongoing formation, as well as discharging their duties to the best of their abilities.

It is hoped that this parish pastoral group will, in due course, evolve into the Parish Pastoral Council.

b) Nomination/Election Model

In almost every parish there is a core group of people exercising a variety of ministries for the good of the whole community, e.g. eucharistic ministers, readers, organists, musicians, sacristans, youth leaders, parents' representatives on school boards, Legion of Mary, St Vincent de Paul, adult religious education, etc.. These different groups are asked to nominate one or two members who will act as a steering committee to coordinate what is already happening in the parish by way of pastoral activity and to plan future directions. Part of their brief is to tap new resources and identify those pastoral areas which are currently being neglected or overlooked.

With a view to discerning pastoral needs, the steering committee prepares and distributes a questionnaire to each parishoner over sixteen years of age. In addition, it asks for nominations of people from their geographical area of the parish who might be prospective members of a pastoral council. If these nominees are willing to be involved, their names will appear on a ballot paper for that area of the parish. Elections are then held for a parish pastoral group, while the priest(s) of the parish are free to nominate some further members to it.

While this process is in progress, the priest(s) of the parish will seize every opportunity to explain to the steering committee, and indeed to the whole parish, what a parish pastoral council is and how it differs from a finance council.

The parish pastoral group will then undertake the preparation and formation course and, in due course, will evolve into a parish pastoral council.

c) The Small Rural Parish Model

Many parishes in rural Ireland cater for small communities of between three and six hundred people. Sometimes a number of these together form the geographical parish. Pastoral scope and the number of people wishing to be actively involved will determine the structure and manner of setting up a pastoral council.

The priest's first task in these circumstances is to identify and list the various organisations functioning within the parish and the ministries being performed by them. His next task is to identify those areas currently being neglected. A meeting of all those currently involved in parish ministry, and of other potential participants, is arranged and the idea of forming a pastoral council is floated. Input on the nature and structure of a pastoral council is provided by a competent facilitator or by someone who has been down this road already. The group is broken into smaller groups, with each smaller group representing a particular area of ministry. Each person is asked to opt for some particular area and in this way those who are already active in a variety of ministries are asked to opt for one of them. In due course the names of those willing to commit themselves to the various areas of pastoral care are balloted on and two people are elected from each panel. Meanwhile the priest is availing of every opportunity to explain to the whole parish the idea of the pastoral council. He himself is free to nominate a few members to the council.

Since we are still very much at the stage of groping in the dark and experimenting, it might be preferable to begin with such councils remaining in office for a period of three years. Members should be eligible to serve two consecutive terms only. There is a lot to be said for staggering the membership so that the whole council is not replaced together.

Constitution

The *Code of Canon Law* stipulates that the parish pastoral council be 'regulated by the norms laid down by the diocesan bishop' (c.536, §1). This would seem to imply that there be some form of standard constitution within the diocese for these councils. Such a constitution would serve to harmonise standards from one parish to the next.

The norms of this constitution should be as simple as possible. The constitution itself might be modelled on that of the council of priests, once the necessary adjustments have been made.

DRAFT CONSTITUTION FOR PARISH PASTORAL COUNCILS

1. *Name*

   The Council shall be called 'The [...] Pastoral Council'.

2. *Nature and Function*

   2.1 The Parish Pastoral Council is a representative body of Christ's faithful whose purpose is the promotion of the mission of the Church in its entirety in this particular corner of the vineyard. It shall at all times work in close collaboration with the priest(s) of the parish, advising him/them in matters pertaining to pastoral ministry (cf. Cs.528-529).

The function of the Pastoral Council is to deal with the mission of the Church, long-range and short-range goals and objectives, and to design those procedures and processes by which the pastoral work of the Church is to be accomplished.

2.2 In accordance with the mind of the Church, the Council shall have a consultative voice only. Through its insights, expertise and prudent advice, it will help the priest(s) identify, implement and evaluate those pastoral initiatives and policies best suited to the spread of the gospel in this particular area (cf. Cs.536§2; 127).

3. *Membership*

3.1 The following shall be *ex officio* members: all priests of the parish (and the parish sister or pastoral assistant, if there is one).

3.2 The priest(s) shall freely co-opt onto the Council not more than five members, noted for their talents, skills or positions they already hold in the parish.

3.3 In so far as is possible, at least one person representing the different areas of pastoral ministry in the parish shall be elected or nominated to the Council. Care should be taken to ensure that different geographical areas, age groups and social classes are represented.

3.4 The Council shall consist of fifteen to twenty members.

4. *Selection of Members*

4.1 Some members of the Council shall be *ex officio*.

4.2 Not less than half the members shall be freely elected by the people of the parish, taking into account the criteria laid down in nos. 3.2-3.3.

4.3 The parish priest may freely appoint some others in accordance with no. 3.2.

5. *Officers*

5.1 The Parish Priest shall be President of the Pastoral Council.

5.2 The Chairperson, whose function is the effective running of meetings, is appointed annually by the members.

5.3 This Pastoral Council shall have a secretary and a treasurer, who are elected by the members. They shall hold these positions for not more than two consecutive years.

5.4 Each sub-committee shall elect from its members a chairperson and a secretary.

6. *Meetings*

6.1 Meetings shall take place four to five times yearly. The parish priest, or another priest of the parish designated by him, shall preside at all meetings. There can be no meeting without the priest.

6.2 Prior to each meeting, the priest, together with the chairperson and secretary, shall draw up the agenda. Members of the Council are invited to submit motions for the agenda The agenda shall include matters pertaining to the mission of the Church, i.e. the full range of pastoral activities which will enable this particular faith-community to listen more attentively to God's word and put it into practice in its day-to-day life.

6.3 Because of the unique nature of the Council, a short period of each meeting shall be given over to prayer and reflection on an appropriate section of God's word.

7. *Period of Membership*

7.1 The period of office shall be three years. No member shall serve more than two consecutive terms but shall be eligible for renomination subsequently.

7.2. Any member failing to attend four consecutive meetings without reasonable explanation shall be deemed to have resigned.

7.3 Vacancies shall be filled by co-option.

8. *Cessation of Council:*
   Since the Council is, by its very nature, advisory to the parish priest, it ceases to exist when the parish becomes vacant.
9. *Quorum*
   A quorum shall consist of half the members of the Council.
10. *Sub-Committees*
    The Council may set up sub-committees to advise it on matters of special pastoral concern. Other people, because of their particular expertise and competence, may be co-opted onto these sub-committees.
11. *Ongoing Formation of Members*
    Study, reflection and inservice education on the nature and mission of the Church is of paramount importance for every member of the Council.
12. *Approval of the Constitution*
    The norms of this Constitution are approved by the Bishop of this diocese.

Suggested further reading:

1. *The New Practical Guide for Parish Councils,* Chpts 8&9, pp 98-131.
2. *Partnership in Parish,* Chpts 6&8, pp 50-64;76-89.
3. Coghlan: 'Team Building' in *Intercom,* May 1989.

PART II

Building a Parish Pastoral Council: A Course of Formation

Introduction

Good pastoral councils don't emerge overnight. They are the product of much effort, toil and sometimes even tears. The reason for this is because they are a new departure or more accurately a new experience of Church. They mark a transition from belonging to the Church to being the Church. Those who are directly involved must be helped to make this transition by suitable prepartion and on-going formation. Preparation is indispensable if the council is to succeed. This prepartion has to take place at two levels:

a) the communication level;
b) the theological and spiritual level.

Ideally, both should go hand-in-hand. What is certain is that neither one can afford to be ignored or bypassed. I will look at each of these areas in turn, paying special attention to the latter.

Communication skills

Ciaran Earley and Gemma McKenna, in their book *Actions Speak Louder*, provide some invaluable insights into the dynamics of group leadership and group-building. No pastoral council should be without a copy of this book. Indeed, in its initial stage of existence, the council might well be advised to seek the assistance of somebody skilled in the area of group facilitation. One does not necessarily have to go to the ends of the earth in search of such a person. In recent years different professional groups have been making wide use of facilitators in in-service training courses for their members. Practically every parish community has people who at some stage will have brushed shoulders with this process, in and through their work or profession. They may be able to lend a helping hand at this precise level.

Enabling people to work together and getting the best out of people is an art in itself. It will pay dividends later. Good will is not enough. It cannot be relied upon when it comes to training and educating people in interpersonal relationships. It takes time, skill and patience to work from people reacting to one another to interacting with each other and being able to detect the difference.

In the event of no facilitator being available, the council itself might usefully embark on a study of selected sections of *Actions Speak Louder* (especially chapters 2 - 7, pp 18 -47) with a view to sharing the authors' suggestions and recommendations with the other members of the council. There they will discover many vignettes of wisdom that we all know so well but yet they seem to evade us when it comes to putting them into practice.

Finally, it should be noted that those who are familiar with the high-powered decision-making of the boardroom are not necessarily the best ones when it comes to using the consultative process. Very often they bring with them the secular model of corporate management where time is money, and economics and profit are the bottom line. Here there is the danger of confusion of roles, misguided agendae, mutual distrust leading to resentment and dissension. If the foundations upon which the whole consultative process rests are shaky, it is difficult to see how it can function effectively. Councils that are currently struggling or experiencing difficulties might well take a further look at the style of leadership out of which they are operating. Ciaran Earley and Gemma McKenna identify three different styles:

1. Enabling Leadership

Here the leader is facilitating the whole group in moving through the commitment process towards the decision. All are advancing together and nobody feels left out or ignored. The decision resulting from this style of leadership carries within itself the momentum and impetus necessary to see it implemented. This style of leadership comes very close to what the post-conciliar Church understands by consultation.

2. Directive Leadership

In this case the leader announces his decision to the group and makes no secret of the fact that he wants the group to concur with it. The council or group is little more than a rubber-stamping apparatus lending respectability to what otherwise might be described as an authoritarian or dictatorial style of leadership. This style may be appropriate when the group is in crisis or starting off or when the decision has already been made and it is merely a matter of administration.

3. Consultative Leadership
Here the leadership makes it clear that it alone will decide the course of action to be pursued at the end of the day, but is interested in picking the brains of the rest of the group for their suggestions and recommendations.

While not being synonomous with the notion consultation as outlined in C. 127§2,2 of the 1983 Code of Canon Law, it does nevertheless enshrine certain elements of it. Consultation, as the Church understands it, is really a mixture of both the enabling and consultative leadership as outlined above.

Theological and spiritual formation
One must be careful not to become bogged down in process, forgetting the primary purpose of the council, namely the mediation of pastoral care to people. To do this effectively people must be acquainted with the mission of the Church and the parish in particular, and possess the spiritual motivation to minister to their brothers and sisters. This is something that can only be achieved through formation and training.

Enda Lyons' book, *Partnership in Parish*, together with its Study Guide, provides an excellent theological grounding for prospective members of a pastoral council. Some adult religious education groups around the country are already using it.

For those who have not had such an opportunity or who feel that they need something more specifically directed to their work as members of a pastoral council I propose a course of formation of six sessions.

Background to Meeting One

Parish as you have experienced it

Purpose of night:
To launch a six-week course of preparation for prospective members of a parish pastoral council.

To explain briefly the topics for consideration each night:
Night 1: Parish as you have experienced it
Night 2: Parish: the continuation of the mission of Christ
Night 3: Parish: towards a vision statement
Night 4: Parish Pastoral Council: its make-up
Night 5: Parish Pastoral Council: consultative body
Night 6: Consultation at work: the Council of Jerusalem

Night 7: First Formal Meeting of The Parish Pastoral Council

To explain the process that will be used each night, i.e. the various steps that will be followed:
Introduction
Focusing Activity
Say your own word
Input
Dialogue
Summary
Task

To introduce the participants to reflection on their own experience of parish.

Meeting One

Personnel: Facilitator, Input Person, Recording Secretary.
Materials: Paper and crayons, personal notebooks, overhead projector.

1. Introduction
Word of welcome from the priest. Opening prayer. Each person introduces him/herself and says a few words about his/her involvement in parish life. The priest explains briefly how this group has come together, what they hope to achieve and the method that will be used.

2. Focusing Activity
Distribute sheets of paper and crayons, and ask each person to draw a sketch of the parish, inserting its main features and symbols of parish life.

3. Say your own word
Divide the participants into groups of four and ask them to share their feelings and views on the following:
  a) What does the word 'parish' mean to you?
  b) Memories and experiences of parish or parishes in which you may have lived.

One person in each group acts as reporter. The facilitator gathers the ideas about parish from the groups and writes them under these headings:
  What is a parish?
  What is it for?

4. Input
The facilitator or Input person presents a short input on the notion of parish today. He/she compares and contrasts a 'people-centred' notion with the older 'territory-centred' idea.

The idea of parish as a 'faith-community' is highlighted, as are also the different styles of parish that different members of the group have encountered. The facilitator endeavours to draw from the group the dominant features of each style of parish, as outlined in chapter 2 above, and helps them to formulate a picture of the different types of parish that can and do exist.

5. Dialogue

The small groups discuss the input and are asked to draw an image of a people-centred parish, inserting symbols to identify the various categories of people within the parish from the point of view of hearing God's word and putting it into practice in their lives.

One person from each group explains the image/diagram in each case to the large group. The facilitator records and orders the observations of each group.

6. Summary

Participants reflect in silence on the main insights they gleaned from the meeting and write these observations into their personal notebooks. With the help of the participants, the Recording Secretary records the principal discoveries of the meeting for recall at the next meeting.

7. Task

Each participant shall complete the following task before the next meeting:

a) write in his/her notebook a description of the ideal (dream) parish.

b) canvass a few neighbours for their views of parish.

8. The meeting ends with a concluding prayer.

Background to Meeting Two

Parish: the continuation of the mission of Christ

Vision

The following extracts will help to focus attention on the meaning and purpose of parish, and how it is envisaged it should function:

> A parish is a certain community of Christ's faithful stably established within a particular Church (i.e. a diocese), whose pastoral care, under authority of the diocesan Bishop, is entrusted to a parish priest as its proper pastor.
> (1983 *Code of Canon Law*, C. 515§1).

The parish priest is not expected to discharge this office of pastoral care single-handedly:

> The pastors indeed know well how much the laity contribute to the welfare of the Church. For they know that they themselves were not established by Christ to undertake alone the whole salvific mission of the Church to the world, but that it is their exalted office to be shepherds of the faithful and also recognise the latter's contribution and charisms that every one in his own way will, with one mind, cooperate in the common task. (*Lumen Gentium*, n. 30)

Pope John Paul II's description of parish:

> The ecclesial community, while always having a universal dimension, finds its most immediate and visible expression in the parish. It is there that the Church is seen locally. In a certain sense it is the Church living in the midst of the homes of her sons and daughters...
> The parish is not principally a structure, a territory or a building, but rather, 'the family of God, a fellowship afire with a unifying spirit', 'a familial and welcoming home'. Plainly and simply the parish is founded on a theological reality, because it is a Eucharistic community... ...the parish is a community of faith and an organic community, that is constituted by ordained ministers and other Christians...

> The lay faithful ought to be ever more convinced of the special meaning that their commitment to the apostolate takes on in their parish...
> The lay faithful should accustom themselves to working in the parish in close union with their priests, bringing to the Church community their own and world problems as well as questions concerning human salvation, all of which need to be examined together and solved through general discussion. As far as possible the lay faithful ought to collaborate in every apostolic and missionary undertaking sponsored by their own ecclesial family.
> The Council's mention of examining and solving pastoral problems 'by general discussion' ought to find adequate and structured development through a more convinced, extensive and decided appreciation for 'Parish Pastoral Councils', on which the Synod Fathers have rightly insisted. (*The Vocation and Mission of the Laity*, nn. 26-27, pp 70-75)

Aim

To help people at the meeting to realise that pastoral care of people is not something that pertains only to the priest but is the shared responsibility of all believers. To help people identify and specify the different areas of pastoral care in the parish.

Process

Review of previous meeting
Introduction
Focusing activity
Say your own word
Input
Dialogue
Summary
Task

Meeting Two

1. Review of previous meeting
The meeting begins with a word of welcome, an opening prayer, a recall of the last meeting, a feedback about tasks undertaken and a sharing of the responses by the participants.

2. Introduction
The introduction to the meeting will explain its objective: i.e. to explore the vision of parish in the post-conciliar Church with a view to making this vision a reality in this particular parish. The facilitator explains what is meant by 'vision' in terms of 'dream' as used by Martin Luther King Jr, 'I have a dream...'

3. Focusing activity
Each person is given a sheet of paper and asked to write down his/her understanding of the vision that Jesus had for people and how he communicated this through his words and action..

4. Say your own word
After a short while, the participants are divided into groups of four and asked to share their insights and give examples from the gospels to substantiate them. One person from each group acts as reporter and the facilitator notes the responses on a flip-chart. People are encouraged to elaborate further to ensure that no aspect of Jesus' ministry is overlooked. The facilitator summarises responses under suitable headings.

5. Input
The facilitator or Input Person explains that the sole purpose of the parish is to promote the spiritual well-being of its members by continuing the mission of Christ in its entirety.(cf. *Partnership in Parish*, pp. 50-55). Pastoral care derives from and is modelled on the example of Christ, the Good Shepherd (Jn 10). The mission of Christ is discussed as:

i. Teacher/Preacher;
ii. Healer/Comforter/Reconciler;
iii. Mediator/Intercessor (i.e.prayer).

6. Dialogue
The groups discuss the input. The following questions will help to focus attention on the objective of the meeting:

How can our parish continue the teaching role of Christ?
Identify the various areas of continuing catechetical need in the parish.
How does our parish continue the healing/reconciling role of Christ?
Identify those groups in the parish needing care, healing and outreach.
How does our parish continue the prayer ministry of Christ?
List the different areas of prayer and worship in parish life.

The group discussion is followed by a dialogue between the facilitator or Input Person and individuals within the group.

7. Summary
Participants reflect in silence to discover the main insights they took from the meeting, and they write these observations into their personal notebooks.

The participants, with the assistance of the facilitator, draw up a comprehensive list of areas of pastoral concern for this parish if it is to be faithful to the mission of Christ in its entirety. These headings are listed on the flip-chart and compared with those areas of concern mentioned in chapter 3 above.

8. Task
These tasks are to be carried out before the next meeting:

a) Each participant is asked to list, in order of priority, six different areas of pastoral mission for the parish.

b) Each participant is asked to canvass the views of two neighbours with a view to determining what would help them to live out the gospel better. The results of this enquiry will be reported and processed at the next meeting.

9. The meeting ends with a short scripture reading and a prayer.

Background to Meeting Three

Towards a vision statement

Vision

'Where there is no vision, people die.' (Proverbs 8:19) The same is true of a parish. Vision is at the heart of every vocation and mission in life. Vision gives us not only the road on which we choose to walk but is also the radiant beacon beckoning us on. It compels us to take a stand on issues just as it did Martin Luther King, Jr.

If this parish is to come alive and fulfill its vocation of leading people to God, it must have a vision. The Irish Catholic Bishops, in their Statement after their Emmaus Meeting in September 1986, present us with a comprehensive vision of parish. The Bishops identify different priorities for the Irish Church:

> The first area is the parish, because it is in the parish that the people experience a sense of belonging to and a sense of participation in the life of the Church. We devoted a lot of time to thinking about the renewal of parish life, the building up of the community, greater participation by lay people in the life of the Church and at parish level. These points emerged:
>
> (i) Bearing in mind that some very good models of parish already exist, we would like to see in every parish in the country pre-sacramental preparation for all parents, for baptism, first confession, holy communion and confirmation.
>
> (ii) We would like to see in every parish in the country a liturgy group to assist the priest in the preparation for Sunday Mass.
>
> (iii) Very much aware of the need that people feel for study and for a deepening of their faith, we would like to see every parish in the country take responsibility for adult religious formation, either on its own or in collaboration with neighbouring parishes.
>
> (iv) We would like to see parish or pastoral councils in every parish where they do not exist.

> (v) Parish visitation by priests, getting to know people in their homes, should be an absolute priority, as should the ministry to special groups, such as handicapped and the sick and the old and the poor and the bereaved.
> To sum it up, every parish should be a place where everybody feels involved, wanted and loved.

The relevant section of the above Statement referring to prayer runs as follows:

> The second area of importance we identified is that of prayer. There is among people, including the young, a hunger for prayer and a desire to know how to pray. The comparative survey of religious practice, attitudes and beliefs (1974-1984), produced for us by the Council for Research and Development last year, indicated this very strongly. Surprisingly enough, perhaps, it also indicated that more people seemed to be praying in 1984 than had been praying a decade before. We see the need for a concerted effort to train people in methods of prayer.

Aim

The aim of this meeting is to enable the group to work out a vision statement for the parish over the next three years. This entails targetting certain areas of pastoral care for immediate attention.

Meeting Three

1. Review of Previous Meeting
The meeting begins with an opening prayer and a word of welcome. It is followed by a short discussion of the areas of pastoral priority that different members have identified and reflected on since the last meeting, as well as those areas adverted to by the people whom they consulted.

2. Introduction
The introduction includes a brief resumé of the mission of the parish, ie. the continuation of the teaching, healing and prayer ministry of Jesus. The purpose of tonights's meeting is to take this process a step further by concretising the mission of the Church in this particular parish right now. In short, the objective of the meeting is to develop a vision statement for this parish for the next three years. The facilitator explains the importance of having a 'vision'.

3. Focusing activity
Each person is given a sheet of paper and asked to write down, in order of priority, those areas of pastoral concern that should figure in a vision statement for the parish.

4. Say your own word
After a short while, the participants are divided into small groups of three or four and asked to share their views on parish pastoral priorities. One person from each group acts a reporter and the facilitator notes the responses on a flipchart .

5. Input
The facilitator or Input person speaks of the need to articulate a vision for the parish that wiil be its guide and inspiration over the next three years. He/she explains the vision of the Irish Bishops for every parish as outlined above. He/she draws on material

from chapter 3 above, which discusses in detail 'The Mission of the Parish'. In particular, he/she invites the participants to select certain areas for immediate attention.

6. Dialogue
The small groups discuss the input and are asked to list five pastoral areas where a start can be made right away. Questions such as the following might be helpful to stimulate and direct the discussion:

How can the quality of our Sunday liturgy be improved?
Is there a real sense of community in the parish?
Are the needs of the sick, the handicapped, the elderly and the bereaved being cared for?

7. Summary
The participants are asked to propose five pastoral priorities which are written up on a flipchart and which will constitute the backbone of a vision statement for the parish.

8. Task
(a) Each participant is asked to reflect on his/her preparedness to become actively involved in the pastoral mission of the parish and to motivate others to do likewise. Such involvement will be demanding in terms of time, energy and spiritual commitment.
(b) Each participant is asked to approach one or two other parishioners whom they think would be interested in getting involved in some particular pastoral activity, if requested.

9. The meeting ends with a short scripture reading and a prayer.

Background to Meeting Four

Parish Pastoral Council: its make-up

Vision

The following extracts from earlier in this book will help to focus attention on what a parish pastoral council is:

> The parish pastoral council is a representative body of the faithful, working in close collaboration with the priest(s) of the parish, with a view to furthering the mission of Christ and his Church in this corner of the Lord's vineyard. It is collegiality in action at parish level.
>
> By its very definition, the parish pastoral council must concern itself with pastoral matters, i.e. the whole range of pastoral activities within the parish.
>
> The purpose of the pastoral planning council is to study the life and activity of the people of God; to research the ideas, the needs, the hopes of the people of God, their actions and so on; secondly to evaluate the parish in conformity with the gospel; and, thirdly, to recommend policies, procedures and programmes.
>
> The job of the parish (pastoral) council is to deal with the mission of the Church, long-range and short-range goals and objectives, and to design those procedures and processes by which the pastoral work of the Church is accomplished.

Aim

To help the participants to become aware of their function as members of a parish pastoral council, with a view to discerning its implications for them and their lifestyles.

Meeting Four

1. Review of the previous meeting

The meeting begins with an opening prayer, a word of welcome and a discussion of the tasks that have been carried out since the last meeting.

The facilitator takes note of the views and the fears that different members will voice with regard to the commitment they are taking on. He re-assures them that it is a team effort and that ultimately it is the Lord who will be working through them.

The facilitator asks that the names of those who have been approached, and who have expressed an interest in becoming involved, be submitted privately at the end of the meeting.

2. Introduction

The introduction includes a brief exposition on the function of a parish pastoral council as highlighted in the above excerpts and a word about the order of tonight's meeting.

3. Focusing activity

The purpose of this activity is to get the participants to focus on themselves – their own needs and faith-commitment and what has helped them to witness to gospel values in their everyday life.

The participants divide into groups of four. Each one picks those statements from the following list which seem to ring a bell with themselves, with a view to sharing it with the group:

1. I find the Sunday Mass boring and unfulfilling. The scripture readings are often unintelligible and have little to say to me.
2. Modern man listens more willingly to witnesses than to teachers; if he is to listen to teachers, it is because they are also witnesses (Pope Paul VI).
3. Belonging to a particular parish means paying one's dues and contributing to collections for renovating the churches and schools – nothing more.
4. I like going to church in parish X because I feel welcome and part of the community.

5. I remember when my mother was dying of cancer. Father X visited her regularly, both in the hospital and at home. He was a great source of strength both to her and to all of us.

6. I was made redundant in my job six months ago and I have little prospect of getting another job. I may have to emigrate.

7. I attended a christening recently – the first in almost twenty years. I was amazed at how much things have changed since my own children were baptised.

8. I find that I'm very well informed on issues of social justice and deprivation in Nicaragua and elsewhere but very slow to advert to injustices in my own parish and neighbourhood, e.g. the plight of the Travelling People.

9. It is very easy to be selective when putting the gospel into practice. We can close our eyes to those things that disturb us and make us feel uncomfortable.

10. The recent debates and referenda on issues like divorce and abortion have left me very confused. We never learned anything about them going to school and so I didn't know what to think when asked to vote on them.

11. I find my parish so large that I always seem to be worshipping with strangers.

12. In the Church all are nourished by each one and each one is nourished by all. (St Gregory the Great.)

4. Say your own word

The groups consider the following question:

What would make our parish more attractive for people intent on living their lives according to gospel values?

The leader in each small group is asked to list those aspects of parish life that would facilitate a more fruitful living out of the gospel.

5. Input

The facilitator or Input Person presents a vision of parish as a 'team effort', taking into account the excerpts above. If a team is to be successful, all the players must be pulling together and putting in their maximum effort. They must also be prepared to put themselves out and be open to ongoing training and formation. This necessarily entails a spiritual component also. A pastoral council is not just a decision-making body that happens to pray, but rather a praying body that makes decisions. In a word, he motivates his team. He uses the diagram on p 42 on an overhead projector in order to highlight the different areas of pastoral care in the average parish.

6. Dialogue
The small groups discuss the input. The following questions will help to focus attention on identifying those areas of pastoral care in which the pastoral council can involve itself immediately:
What areas did our neighbours draw attention to when we canvassed their views on parish life?
What areas surfaced most frequently in your own group sharing, earlier on this evening, when you reflected on the ten points distributed at the start of the meeting?
Is there anything that was missed out, in light of the input?

7. Summary
The participants are asked to reflect in silence on the pastoral priorities that have been identified and agreed upon. They are also asked to reflect on their own faith-commitment and on what will be expected of them in terms of Christian living etc..

8. Task
a) Each participant is asked to think of two people who they reckon have talents which could be used for the good of the whole Christian community. This is with a view to establishing a number of sub-committees who would take responsibility for different pastoral initiatives in the parish.
b) Each participant is asked to write down for the next night their experience and evaluation of some committee meeting at which he/she was present and which appeared to run smoothly and effectively.

9. The meeting concludes with a reading from 1Cor 12:4-11, followed by a short prayer.

Background to Meeting Five
Parish Pastoral Council: consultative body

Vision

It is through the avenue of consultation that decisions are arrived at in the Church. This is the form of decision-making appropriate to the Church as a hierarchical communion. The Church is neither a democracy nor a monarchy but encompasses elements of both in its visible structure. In arriving at decisions it tries to take both these factors into account.

From the beginning, the Church has operated this procedure in reaching decisions. When a dispute arose in the early Church over a pastoral matter – the distribution of food to the poor – the Twelve called a full meeting of the disciples and proposed to them to select seven men to look after this matter. The whole community approved of this proposal (Acts 6:1-6). This was consultation in action. Consensus was arrived at without having recourse to voting.

A fuller discussion of the notion of consultation is to be found in chapter 5 above and in C.127 of the *Code of Canon Law*.

Aim

The aim of this meeting is to explore the consultative process and how it operates in practice.

Process

To take a particular topic, totally unrelated to pastoral matters, and work it through to the point of making a decision on it. The same steps are followed as at previous meetings.

Meeting Five

1. Review of the previous meeting

The meeting begins with a word of welcome and an opening prayer. The Recording Secretary recalls the highlights of the last meeting. The participants are invited to report back on the tasks undertaken.

The facilitator explains briefly that the parish is a community of faith and hence differs radically from any business or political organisation with which we might be familiar. It arrives at its decision, not by voting, but by consensus.

2. Focusing activity

The participants divide into groups of four and each person is asked to reflect on the following questions and to write some observations in his/her notebook.

a) What, in your experience, is the key to running a successful meeting?

b) In your experience of committee meetings, who are the people who wield the most influence in determining the course of action that is eventually taken?

3. Say your own word

In the small groups, the participants share their reflections on those questions. They are invited above all to listen to each other's observations.

The facilitator takes feedback.

4. Input

The facilitator or Input Person explains the notion of a consultative vote and how it contrasts with a deliberative vote. It is particularly emphasised that 'making-the-choice' is only a very small part of the decision-making process. The various stages involved in decision-making are outlined, as well as the meaning of consensus. These stages are written up on a flip-chart or shown on an overhead projector.

5. Dialogue
The small groups discuss the input. They use the consultative process in reaching a decision on 'The merits of establishing a tennis club in the parish'.

The group discussion is followed by a general discussion with the Input Person. In particular, the group tries to identify the qualities and skills required in those committed to operating this process.

6. Summary
a) Reflect in silence to discover the main insights gleaned from this meeting.

b) The Recording Secretary notes these for recall at subsequent meetings.

7. Task
a) List in your personal notebook four areas of pastoral priority for your parish right now, i.e. areas to which the pastoral council can address itself right away.

b) Enlist the support of a number of friends or neighbours to pray for the success of the pastoral initiatives that will be undertaken by the parish pastoral council.

Background to Meeting Six

Consultation at Work: the Council of Jerusalem

Vision

Consultation is the standard process invoked by the Church when searching out solutions to problems arising out of pastoral practice. In this process, the manner of arriving at the decision is as important as the content of the decision. The Council of Jerusalem, in 50 A.D., (Acts 15:1-35) provides a perfect example of this process in action. Before one can appreciate the process used in arriving at a solution, one must first have a clear grasp of the problem.

The problem arose out of the influx of Gentiles into the Church. Jewish Christians felt that non-Jews could only become Christians by first becoming Jews, i.e. by being circumcised and accepting the Law of Moses. Needless to say, this view was not shared by non-Jews. The climate was ripe for disagreement and discord, but the Christian community realised that it could not allow itself to be split into factions on a matter of fundamental policy. So the apostles and elders met in Jerusalem to look into the matter, and after much debate (v.7) a solution was finally proposed which won the approval of all (v. 22).

Aim

The aim of this meeting is to examine the consultative process in action in the early Church, with a view to it being adopted by this group.

Process

To relive the Council of Jerusalem within this group and thereby experience the dynamics at work within the consultative process. The basic steps are similar to those used at previous meetings.

Meeting Six

1. Review of the previous meeting
The meeting begins with a word of welcome and an opening prayer. The Recording Secretary recalls the highlights of the previous meeting.

2. Focusing activity
The participants are divided into groups of three or four and each one is given a copy of Acts 15:1-35 and asked to reflect on it and answer the following questions in their personal notebooks:

What was the final solution to the controversy and who proposed it?
Which side could lay claim to victory – the Jewish Christians or the Gentile Christians?
What was the role of the Church leaders (Paul, Barnabas, Peter and James) in resolving this dispute?

3. Say your own word
The participants share their observations in the small groups and one of them reports back at the feedback.

4. Input
The facilitator focuses more closely on the text of Acts 15:1-35. In particular he/she draws attention to the place of listening in the whole process. He notes the verses in the text: 'This silenced the entire assembly and they listened to Barnabas and Paul...' (v. 12) who were reporting on factual happenings, not feelings. He highlights the obstacles to attentive listening (cf. *Actions Speak Louder*, pp 41-43.)

Finally, he draws attention to the person who exercises most influence in determining the outcome of the Council. It was James. He was the last to speak. He was a respected figure, the leader of the Jerusalem church. His was a moral leadership, based not on authority but rather on a deep sensitivity and respect for the feelings of the Jews and Gentiles alike. He proposes a solution acceptable to both sides and that wins the approval of all.

5. Dialogue

The small groups discuss the input with a view to making some concrete proposals about the running and operation of future parish pastoral council meetings.

The group discussion is followed by a general discussion with the input person or facilitator. The main proposals emerging are written up on a flip-chart or shown on an overhead projector.

6. Summary

a) Reflect in silence on the essential ingredients of the consultative process as used at the Council of Jerusalem.

b) The Recording Secretary notes these for recall at the next meeting, the first meeting of the Parish Pastoral Council.

7. Task

List in your personal notebook those areas or aspects of the consultative process which you expect to find:

a) most difficult to implement;

b) easiest to implement.

8. The meeting ends with a reading of Acts 15: 22-29 – the implementation of the decision reached – and a prayer.

The first formal meeting of the Parish Pastoral Council

Purpose of meeting

1. To give the newly constituted Council a name.
(cf. *Draft Constitution for Parish Pastoral Councils)*
2. To elect officers in accordance with no. 5.
3. To select sub-committees (n.5.2.) which will explore and respond to the different pastoral needs which have been identified during the preparatory meetings.
4. To decide the dates and frequency of subsequent meetings of the Council.
5. To establish an agenda committee and determine the manner of getting items on to the agenda for discussion (6.2).
6. To determine the form and nature of ongoing spiritual and theological formation that the Council will undertake during the coming year (n.11), e.g. a study of select passages from the book *Partnership in Parish* , as well as occasional evenings of prayer and reflection.
7. To draw up a provisional Constitution which will be submitted to the Bishop for approval (n.12).

Process

Each of the officers assume their office as soon as elected. During the course of formation, different members will have emerged as suitable for particular roles within the council.

PART III

The Maintenance of a Parish Pastoral Council

The function of the Chairperson

The function of the chairperson is to aid the listening process by clarifying, summarising and paraphrasing what has already been said. His/her task is to encourage the other members to express their point of view. Questions are a chairperson's greatest ally and aid. Use of good questions at the appropriate moment can transform heat into light. Questions are a good way of encouraging the shy and of halting the garrulous. It is inevitable that some strong and overpowering people will make their way onto the pastoral council. The chairperson has to contend with them also. He/she must be scrupulous in recognising minority views while at the same time forestalling division and rancour among members. Ultimately it is the chairperson who is the custodian of the group. Ensuring that the council does not get sidetracked and bogged down in trivia is part of this function.

The chairperson is primarily a facilitator. He/she is charged with providing the process whereby the group can discuss its subject in the most fruitful and satisfactory way possible. This involves a twofold role, namely: that of ensuring that the group achieves the goals and tasks it sets itself, while at the same time maintaining a good spirit within the group. At all stages in the life of the council the chairperson has to keep this double end in view.

The authors of *Actions Speak Louder* set out very clearly the dual role of the facilitator or chairperson. As already noted, he/she has both a task-job and a maintenance-job to do. The following guidelines, which rely heavily on those proposed by Ciaran Earley and Gemma McKenna, will help the chairperson of a group dedicated to the consultative process:

Task	*Maintenance*
1.*Initiating*: Opening the discussion on a topic,	*Encouraging*: Inviting others to express their

outlining its context and parameters, e.g: rationalising the number of Sunday Masses in a parish. This is the creative idea stage (cf. p 23 above).	views; being open, friendly and reassuring.
2. *Gathering the information*: Eliciting the factual information available and identifying further useful sources. This is the fact finding stage (cf. p 50 above).	*Gatekeeping*: Bringing the quiet person into the discussion and halting the garrulous.
3. *Sharing the information*: Ensuring that all are aware of the facts. Bad decisions are the result of ignorance of the facts.	*Diagnosing difficulties*: Adverting to hidden agendas between members; becoming aware of the need for extra information before proceeding further.
4. *Hearing opinions*: Ensuring that all views are heard, especially those of the minority.	*Taking the pulse of the group*: Perceiving and articulating the feelings of the group: boredom, frustration. Closing the discussion on a minor or trivial issue; refocusing attention on the central issue.
5. *Harmonising*: Helping those in conflict to understand one another's points of view.	*Explaining and clarifying*: Giving practical examples to illustrate a point, asking questions such as: 'Am I right in thinking?' 'It seems to me...' etc.

6.*Evaluating*: Enabling the group to see how it is working together as a group;highlighting what has already been achieved.

Summarising: Stating briefly the main points made so far.

7.*Relieving tension*: Spotting tension building up between members and being able to diffuse it.

Checking consensus: Testing the level of agreement on the topic under discussion.

Fr David Coghlan SJ, a Process Consultant, who teaches at the College of Industrial Relations in Dublin, in a series of succinct articles in *Intercom*, provides some very valuable insights and hints for the running of more productive meetings. He gives some useful rules-of-thumb for managing a meeting, which no chairperson can afford to ignore:

1. Start on time. Don't train people to be late.
2. Begin by reviewing the purpose of the meeting.
3. Decide how long the meeting will last.
4. Review the agenda and set priorities.
5. Stick to the topic under discussion.
6. Avoid long speeches and monologues. They de-energise.
7. Involve as many as possible in the discussion.
8. Keep track of points, decisions reached, etc..
9. Finish on time.

(cf. 'Meetings 2', *Intercom*, May 1988, pp 11-12).

Fr Coghlan also outlines various styles for conducting a meeting and the different techniques that can be used when the group is getting bogged down or seems to have run out of ideas.

Learning to Listen

The effective functioning of the consultative process rests very much on attentive listening. It is the key to its success.

Few of us are good listeners. When a person is speaking, most of us are so busy thinking about our own ideas and how we might respond to some issue raised by the speaker, that we miss most of what is being said. In the book *Actions Speak Louder*, Ciaran Earley and Gemma McKenna make the interesting observation that 'most people think four times as fast as the average person speaks. That means that when someone is talking to us for one minute, we have three quarters of a minute of spare thinking time'(p 41).

Building a listening community is one of the most crucial tasks for the council. Failure to do so defeats the whole purpose of its existence. Time spent on developing listening skills is time well spent. One way of guaranteeing subsequent conflict, inefficiency and frustration is to overlook the need for developing this skill.

Learning to listen is something that grows gradually within a group. It develops hand-in-hand with a growing sense of trust between members and respect for each other.

It is good to be aware of those factors that impede our listening ability. In general it may be said that these factors are either physical or psychological or perhaps a combination of both.

A suitable physical environment is of utmost importance. A large, cold and spartan meeting room in the basement of the church or presbytery compares very unfavourably with the comfort of boardrooms and meeting places that many of our council members are familiar with from secular life. The meeting place should be inviting and conducive to good communication. It should facilitate face-to-face contact between the participants because communication is not just verbal. Actions, postures, gestures and facial expressions betray our convictions and feelings much more clearly than our words do.

According to the experts 55% of communication happens through visual means or appearances. The eyes, we are told are the doorways to the soul. 38% of communication occurs through the tone of one's voice. The same words can convey very different meanings depending on the tone of our voice as we speak them. Only 7% of communication happens through the actual content of the message itself.

At a psychological level, the chief obstacles to attentive listening are the individual's needs and prejudices. As we negotiate our way through the slings and arrows of life, we accumulate an array of hurts and wounds. These in turn create needs within us and shape our prejudices. A person's need for self-esteem can be so great as to make it impossible for him/her to appreciate the point of view of another. Likewise, a person may find it difficult to transcend prejudices. These prejudices may be centred on certain people or topics. When these topics come up in discussion, or when certain people voice their views, invisible barriers begin to appear. These barriers impede attentive listening.

Ciaran Earley and Gemma McKenna draw attention to those factors which obstruct and reduce our listening capacity. In addition, they suggest some useful exercises to develop our listening skills (cf. *Actions Speak Louder*, pp 38-47).

Conflict

Conversion to the consultative process, despite the best intentions, does not come easily to either priests or people. Every pastoral council must expect an element of conflict and misunderstanding. A good facilitator/chairperson can manage tension and disagreement so as to produce even better decisions.

Handling conflict

Before one can handle conflict effectively, one must first understand its dynamics. Conflict arises when one person's self-esteem is threatened. Two people may disagree on a host of issues, but this disagreement only turns into conflict when the integrity or self-esteem of one of the parties is threatened. The person who feels threatened then succumbs unconsciously to the old belief that attack is the best form of defence. Conflict is born, and the relationship between the embroiled parties begins to be in jeopardy.

When conflict arises in a group:

1. The group can *deny* its existence by ignoring it, in the vain hope that it will resolve itself. In the presence of real conflict this is but wishful thinking.

2. It can ***avoid*** it by steering clear of those areas which are calculated to provoke it. Neither is this realistic because it limits the field of discussion to what are considered safe topics.
3. The alternative to these two reactions is ***conflict management.***

In their book, *Collaborative Ministry*, Loughlan Sofield and Carroll Juliano distinguish clearly between conflict resolution and conflict management:

> Many people approach conflict with the desire to resolve it, remove it and reinstate harmony. To expect to achieve this goal in all circumstances is unrealistic. While conflict resolution is possible, conflict management is often more realistic. Managing conflict means being able to live and work together even though the source of conflict has not been eliminated. (p 103)

Different kinds of conflict

But whether one seeks to resolve it or to manage it, the first step is to identify the source and origin of the conflict. It may result from a difference of opinion about facts, objectives or values.

The pastoral council, for instance, is discussing redecorating the youth club facilities. Conflict arises over the cost. This matter can be easily resolved by getting further information and studying what is feasible. Here the matter being disputed is not whether or not the youth club should be redecorated, but merely the issue of getting the best value for money. This type of conflict is the easiest to manage and resolve because it merely concerns facts. The quality of the final decision can be directly enhanced because of the conflict.

But conflict can also arise over objectives or methods for arriving at an agreed goal. The pastoral council, for instance, cannot reach any agreement on the value of the youth club as an effective instrument of pastoral care of young people. Some members are advocating its closure because of allegations of alcohol or drug abuse, while others are in favour of its retention. Here the conflict is at the level of objectives. All the members are genuinely concerned for the pastoral care of youth, but there is no consensus as to the best methods for achieving this. This kind of conflict can often be satisfactorily resolved by getting more knowledge of what is available in the whole area of youth ministry today. What the council needs, perhaps, is to learn about alternative forms of youth ministry, as well as other youth clubs which are seen to be functioning satisfactorily. In this case the cause of the conflict has been isolated and the road to resolving it is already hopefully in sight. Had there been no disagreement, a decision of lesser quality would almost certainly have resulted.

Finally, conflict may arise at the level of values. A value is a reality that is highly prized by an individual and acts as a kind of co-ordinate or internal force in determining the manner in which a person lives and acts. Christian values arise from the life and message of Jesus Christ and from the tradition he set in motion when he called his first disciples.

Different members of the council, because of their age, religious upbringing and experience, will have appropriated the Christian message in different ways. Certain aspects of the Christian message may be very dear to some (Sunday Mass, regular reception of the Sacraments, etc), while others preoccupy them only very marginally (justice issues, etc). Some may be operating out of a pre-conciliar model of Church as a hierarchical institution while others subscribe to the conciliar idea of the Church as the community of God's people trying to discern God's will and to put it into practice in their lives. A further complicating factor is that not all members will have internalised the Christian message to the same degree; they may be at different points in their own faith-journey. An individual may find him/herself locked within the limitations of one or other of these perspectives. The skilled facilitator/chairperson should be able to spot this.

Conflict at the level of values is the most difficult of all to manage. This is because values are part of a person's make-up and compromising on a deeply held value is like self-betrayal.

Conflict arises at the level of values when a person sees no reason for youth ministry as such, not to mention the redecoration of the premises. This person is convinced that youth should be formed in the home and school and that setting up an elaborate youth ministry programme in the parish is an invitation to parents to abdicate their own responsibilities.

The best way of handling this type of conflict is to reduce it to the level of goals or facts. Although knowledge in itself is no guarantee that a person's values will change (if it did, we would have long ago solved the problem of smoking, and be well on the road to containing the spread of AIDS!), it is nevertheless a first step. This means stating clearly the facts and objectives, e.g. parents today feel helpless when it comes to guiding and directing their children, because of the many pressures confronting the young people; they need to be assisted in this task by the resources of the whole christian community.

Conflict at the level of values can be a highly emotive issue. It is the task of the facilitator/chairperson to diffuse its emotional content, to transform heat into light. Sofield and Juliano give some useful hints on managing this type of conflict:

> The goal is to move people from the heart to the head, where some clarity emerges, to the mouth where the people involved are able to dialogue. They need to discover that they are allies, not adversaries. Obtaining emotional distance from the conflict can be accomplished by taking some time away from the meeting and suggesting a few questions for reflection and prayer. The questions should challenge the participants to think about themselves, the cause of the conflict and some of the reasons for the intensity of their feelings.
> (*Collaborative Ministry*, pp 113-114.)

It may be useful for the group leader to have a selection of scripture texts available which would help the council to reflect on its mission of service to the whole parish community and on the manner in which it should execute this mission. I would suggest the following:

1 Cor 4:1-13 Servants in the Lord's vineyard;
1 Cor 12: 4-11 One Church, many ministries;
2 Cor 5:16-21 Ambassadors for Christ;

Eph 4:1-8;11-16 A call to unity;
Col 3:12-17 Forgive each other;
Acts 15:1-35 Consensus in decision-making.

Confidentiality and Dissemination of Information
The observance of confidentiality is required of every board or committee. The parish pastoral council is no exception. Every pastoral council should remind its members from time to time of their obligations in this regard. A council simply cannot function without the guarantee of confidentiality. Members will be reluctant to speak their minds or even get involved in discussions if there is the risk of what they say or think being reported outside the confines of the meeting room. Hence, what individual members say or think about particular items on the agenda should be strictly confidential.

Confidentiality, however, must not be confused with secretiveness. The latter can be equally damaging. It breeds suspicion and runs the risk of the council being seen as another closed shop or elitist kind of group. Since the pastoral council exists for the people of the parish and not for itself, it must do everything to keep all the people both informed and involved in its activities. Besides, not to be informed leaves those charged with implementing the decisions arrived at devoid of any enthusiasm for doing so. Hence, I would suggest that the council devise some way of communicating its deliberations by way of a bulletin or newsletter.

Helping Parish Pastoral Councils grow
Any living body or organism must grow if it is to survive. A pastoral council is no exception. The council must constantly be renewing itself and endeavouring to keep abreast with Church thinking and teaching on particular matters. Ongoing formation is vital. Familiarisation with official Church documents on relevant topics should be among the primary objectives of every pastoral council. Otherwise the council runs the risk of being out of tune with official policy and doing its own thing.

The Role of the Diocese

The working out of pastoral strategy is not something that the council can do in isolation and without reference to the diocese, or indeed the universal Church. If parish pastoral councils are to grow and flourish the diocese must be seen to be in favour of them and actively to promote them.

Some dioceses in Canada and the United States have set up teams with the specific mandate of promoting and directing pastoral councils. They get them off the ground, evaluate them, provide various resources for them, and even assist them to begin again after periods of stagnation. Members of these teams are also available to work with particular councils on particular occasions or projects.

But the diocesan input does not stop when the councils are established. Some dioceses provide an informational and liaison bulletin specifically for members of pastoral councils. This aims at updating the members and making them aware of the pastoral initiatives being taken elsewhere in the diocese and the Church. Other dioceses sponsor a day of spiritual retreat and/or on-going formation in some area of ministry for members. The scope is endless in this field. All that is needed is a few committed and energetic organisers. This would be a most obvious and worthwhile task for a few members of the diocesan pastoral council.

Suggested further reading:

1. *Collaborative Ministry,* Chpts 7&8, pp 101-123.
2. Avery Dulles: *Models of Church*, Chpts 2&3, pp31-57.
3. *The New Practical Guide for Parish Councils* (pp 149-157.)
4. *Collaborative Ministry*, Chpt 6, pp 83-100.
5. David Coghlan SJ: 'A Question of Process' in *Intercom*, June 1987, p 11; 'Meetings 1: How to make effective use of them' in *Intercom*, April 1988, p 8; 'Meetings 2' in *Intercom*, May 1988, pp 11-12.
6. *Actions Speak Louder*, Chpt 18, pp 126-129.

Bibliography

The books suggested for further reading throughout this Handbook are listed at the end of each section by title only. The full bibliographical details are as follows:

The Code of Canon Law	Collins, London, 1983;
A. Flannery OP (Ed)	Vatican Council II, Vol. I: *Conciliar and Post-Conciliar Documents.*(1975) Vatican Council II, Vol. II: *More Post-Conciliar Documents.*(1982) *Both* Dominican Publications, Dublin
John Paul II	*The Vocation and Mission of the Laity,* Veritas Publications, Dublin, 1989.
Enda Lyons	*Partnership in Parish,* The Columba Press, Dublin, 1987.
William Rademacher with Marliss Rogers	*The New Practical Guide for Parish Councils,* XXIII/Columba, Dublin, 1987.
Loughlan Sofield and Carroll Juliano	*Collaborative Ministry,* Ave Maria Press, Indiana, 1987.
Ciaran Earley and Gemma McKenna	*Actions Speak Louder,* The Columba Press, Dublin, 1987.
Michael Paul Gallagher	*Struggles of Faith*, The Columba Press, Dublin, 1990.
William J. Bausch	*Ministry: Traditions, Tensions, Transitions,* 1982. *Hands-on Parish*, 1989. *Both* XXIII/Columba, Dublin.
Joseph M. Champlin	*The Marginal Catholic*, Ave Maria Press, Indiana, 1989.
USCCB	*The Parish: a People, a Mission, a Structure*, Washington D.C., 1980.
Karl Rahner	*Theological Investigations,* Vol 19, *Faith and Ministry*, DLT, London, 1983.
Avery Dulles, S.J.	*Models of the Church*, Gill and Macmillan, Dublin, 1976.
Joseph Martos	*The Catholic Sacraments,* Message of the Sacraments, Vol. 1, Michael Glazier, Wilmington, Delaware, 1983.